AWAKEN TO
EMBRACE
VULNERABILITY
AND SEXUALITY

AWAKEN TO EMBRACE VULNERABILITY AND SEXUALITY

Copyright © 2024, Marcela Onyx.

ISBN: 978-1-7394636-2-5 Paperback

Published by: Inspired By Publishing

Cover Design and Formatting by: Marcela Onyx and Tanya Grant, The TNG Designs Group Limited

Disclaimer:

The information provided in this book is intended to be used for educational and self-help purposes, to offer helpful advice and guidance on personal growth and self-improvement. However, the content is not for diagnosis, prescription, or treatment of any health disorders or intended to replace medical or healthcare professional advice, diagnosis, or treatment. The author and publisher are not responsible for any adverse effects or actions taken based on the information contained in this book. The reader is solely responsible for their own decisions and actions. The techniques, strategies, and suggestions presented in this book are not intended to diagnose or treat any medical, psychological, or emotional conditions. Readers are encouraged to seek the advice of a qualified professional for any concerns they may have.

AWAKEN TO EMBRACE VULNERABILITY AND SEXUALITY

A JOURNEY IN STRENGTHENING YOUR INTIMATE RELATIONSHIP

MARCELA ONYX

My heart sings with gratitude as I reflect on the journey that led me here, to this moment, writing my very first book, which is **dedicated to my soulmate Angelo**. A passionate and devoted husband and father who trusted me twice with the mission to raise our two beautiful children, whom I love and care with all my energy for both of us.

Angelo saw my potential and supported me wholeheartedly. He always believed in my ability to make a difference in the world and encouraged me to pursue my dreams, and supported me, as he would say, being the mother and the father when I had to travel to dedicate quality time to study and develop my personal and spiritual journey as part of my soul's purpose that he knew was meant to be.

Together, we embraced every emotion that life brought our way. We cried tears of both sorrow and joy, felt frustration and anger, but also found happiness, love, and excitement. We supported each other through it all on the happy and toughest time in our relationship without letting each other give up, finding ways to embrace healing and overcoming our struggles. We took our time to savour every moment and to dive deep into the depths of our souls, learning and growing together along the way. We also unfolded our spirituality together, which, after I found inner peace with my grief, allowed us to carry on living our love on a soul and spiritual level, and it has been an amazing experience.

Dear Seeker,

I appreciate your interest in this book. Everyone has the right to be happy and feel good about themselves. To find happiness within, you first need to choose to accept yourself for who you are right now.

I have worked with many people who face complications in relationships with themselves or others because they are uncomfortable being open and vulnerable.

This book will help you awaken to intimacy, vulnerability, and sexuality. It will help you start a journey where you can choose to let go of your resentments and learn and evolve from them. It will also ignite the flame of passion in you so that you work towards happiness and fulfilment. It will teach you ways to accept yourself in your own skin because that's what makes you beautiful.

Make the most of the Self-reflection spaces and use this book as YOUR workbook to reflect, explore and embrace your journey in strengthening your intimate relationship with yourself and your partner.

Any healthy relationship starts with doing our inner work. When we feel comfortable and confident exploring and learning how we want to express and communicate with healthy boundaries, we feel sexually empowered. We can prioritise things that matter to us. Throughout this book, I will inspire you to have your voice for your choices, own your sexuality, and acknowledge your desires without feeling guilty or ashamed. More than that, I will take you through how to spice up your awakening so you can enjoy the passion and in-depth connection with your new happy self or partner.

Healing and transformation take time. Please make a note of these moments and acknowledge them as a powerful tool. While reading this book, please consider how these chapters resonate with you and potentially within your relationships.

Now let's embrace this journey.

Index

CHAPTER 1

The Courage to Connect and Transform

Embarking on a journey of strengthening your intimate relationship with yourself is a bold and courageous step towards unlocking the deepest levels of love, connection, discovery and intimacy we can undertake, regardless of whether we are single or in a relationship.

Taking the time to explore our own intimate desires, wants and needs, both sexually and emotionally, can be an incredibly empowering experience and an important part of self-discovery and personal growth. It allows us to understand ourselves on a deeper level, recognise our own worth and value, and cultivate a sense of self-acceptance and self-love as we learn to embrace all aspects of ourselves, including those that may have been previously hidden, repressed or suppressed. By doing so, we can free ourselves from the constraints of shame, fear, self-doubt and embrace a more authentic and purposeful life, which is essential for building healthy and fulfilling relationships with others.

As we continue on your transformational intimacy journey, we may find that old patterns and beliefs that no longer serve us begin to fall away, allowing us to step into a new way of being in our relationships.

This journey of self-discovery can be empowering and transformative, allowing us to become more confident and comfortable in our own skin. It can also help us to form deeper and more meaningful connections with ourselves and others as we learn to identify and communicate our desires and boundaries effectively.

We all want and deserve love and intimacy and to be in a relationship where we feel seen, heard, and understood. We all have expectations, and most of us think we are outstanding in reading other people's minds, but this can lead to unhelpful assumptions, criticism, judgment, and misunderstandings that can result in a feeling of negative emotions.

No matter what we've been through in the past, we have the power to heal and transform ourselves. Although it may feel scary to revisit painful memories, we can choose to face them with courage and compassion. By embracing the healing process, we can release ourselves from the grip of the past and find inner peace.

As we work through our wounds and challenges, we eventually learn to accept and forgive ourselves and others. We gain valuable insights and wisdom from our experiences, and we grow stronger and more resilient in the process. We let go of the need to blame ourselves or others and instead take responsibility for our own happiness.

We have the capacity to learn, reprogram our minds, change our emotional, mental, and physical states and access fascinating new aspects of ourselves, for example, changing our mindset from one of shame to one of self-compassion and realising that we have a voice. And when we identify what has been holding us back and choose to give a more empowering meaning and create a new reality, we can transform and have meaningful connections that can be more profound, not just with ourselves but also with our relationships.

Several factors may have prevented us from embracing ourselves intimately and even our sexual self to uncover the nature of our sexual relationship and understand how our sexual self-aligns with who we are and how comfortable we are accessing every sexual aspect of ourselves.

Have you ever asked yourself:

"What does my critical inner voice tell me about sex?

Do I know what I like and do not like?

What are my rules, expectations, and boundaries where relationships, self-pleasure, desires, personal values, and sexuality is concerned?

What's wrong with me? Why have I lost interest in being intimate with myself or my partner? Why have I never had an orgasm?

How comfortable and practical do I feel talking to others openly?"

They are deep questions, and most of my clients would say they would like to work on them when we discuss relationships, connection, and intimacy.

Intimacy is "into me I see" or, in other words, "I'm here; see me, hear me." It is an evolving process that encourages you to become more and more conscious of yourself and your surroundings. It brings us closer to connecting with everything so we can dive deeper into ourselves.

Self-knowledge includes developing awareness of your thoughts, opinions, beliefs, feelings, emotions, personality traits, values, needs, goals, preferences, behavioural patterns, fears, triggers, relationships, and social identity.

Intimacy can evoke strong emotions and feelings. It is normal to feel some hesitation when opening up to another person. Some people may have had unpleasant experiences in their sexual life that caused a fear of intimacy, and they may feel apprehension when it comes to getting close to someone else out of the fear of being hurt, rejected, or left alone. People with this fear may feel uncomfortable getting too close to others and withdraw from social situations or intimate relationships.

When you have self-knowledge, you can use that information to make better choices and improve your relationships and intimacy.

The more we learn about ourselves, the more likely we feel empowered to pursue amazing life experiences, creating an inner world where we can enjoy the journey and grow.

To begin an intimate relationship with someone, we must understand ourselves, what we want and desire in our lives, and who we want to be. Because personal intimacy only works when two people are willing to lower their defences and reveal their genuine selves while creating a safe environment for the other to do the same. It takes a lot of courage to build intimacy with another person.

Through my journey of awakening and transformation, I have learned how to live in alignment, embracing a life where I can honestly feel the power of love, joy, authenticity, and immense gratitude for being, living, and working on my purpose. I am in a privileged position where I can support others with love, compassion, empathy, and the right intentions. I can make a difference in their awakening and growth journey.

As I have written this book focusing on supporting you in your awakening journey to strengthening your intimate relationship and embrace vulnerability and sexuality, I feel I would also love to open up and share a transformational journey that gave me experience and inspiration to support others heal struggles with their relationships and write this book that can help you with your own awakening journey to having a confident, sexy and happy intimate life with yourself or your partner.

A lot has happened and transformed my life before I am where I am today. I grew up trying to find where I belonged, Who Am I, why I was adopted, why my adoptive family always felt like blood, we have this loving connection and even look like each other, and why I have been through so many challenges in my life.

As a teenager, I suffered from bullying and body shaming and grew up without being able to talk about my emotions. I had no knowledge about the menstrual cycle until it happened, and I can't even describe the bloody scene. My Mum had a smile on her face when I told her how I was feeling so scared and asked my older cousin to explain what was happening to me.

Most women reading this may remember their first period and how that forever changes their lives and innocence.

My first visit to the gynecologist was at the age of fifteen and quite traumatic, to be honest, as once again, I had no clue what would happen. I just knew I hated experiencing heavy menstrual cycles that would cause me sickness and headaches (my Mum thought I was making excuses to miss college). The trauma was related to how the exam would took place, without being told what was about to happen, how the exam would take place, why I had to go through it all, and the fact that I had a few spectators; not only was my Mum there, but I had a male gynecologist, and we also had two nurses looking between my legs... I guess now you can understand the pain and shame that the young version of me felt going through that situation, which happened without my consent. Well, talking about sex was also a tabu, funny enough not even the gynaecologist had this conversation with me, maybe because he also felt my Mum was conservative. However, looking back in time, I think I immensely appreciate that I had been part of a generation that grew up with strong family values, simplicity and innocence.

Where relationships are concerned, I had trust issues. The oldest always thought they knew better than me and could not say a word or, according to my culture, would be a lack of respect. As I got older, I just got used to being very straightforward, and yes, I had suffered a lot with people's opinions and judgment when all I was doing was expressing myself authentically. Nowadays, I am happy to inspire others to be heard, to be seen, and share my messages with the world.

I haven't changed much since turning twenty-one. My Mum finally acknowledged that I was an adult and deserved the freedom to travel and live my life without her tough love. As an adult, I've come to realize that she helped me to the best of her knowledge and abilities, having grown up with even stricter parents who worked hard on the land to provide for the family.

From the healing that I have done, I understood a beautiful lesson, we all want love and to feel loved, but only each of us can know what love means to us, what we may expect from someone to do or say to us that will reassure us and make us feel loved by them without it being just words.

Please remember to be kind and empathise with others that may not meet your expectations. Remember that they are yours and not theirs; everyone has a different story and background, some histories may even sound similar, but we are not in each other's skin to know how they feel, and some people may not be able to meet others' expectations because they had never experienced any different, we all feel insecure when we deal with unfamiliar situations. Some people may look in their relationships for similar traits that their parents had in a positive or negative way. It's important to disassociate, heal blockages and feel the freedom to be your authentic self in life and with relationships.

My personality never stopped me from having meaningful relationships; I still have friends from school, college, and university times present in my life, plus amazing friends all over the globe and friends that are like soul family.

At the age of twelve, I remember starting to accumulate love letters, but I never sent any. I never liked or loved any of those boys. I felt bad for not being able to correspond with their expectation. I had accumulated admirers in love with me, and my Mum would always say that she did not want to know anyone coming to our door after school and that I was too young to date.

I learned a lot from my first dating experience. I started working and dating at the age of sixteen, and it lasted for five years. My first boyfriend is still a very close friend of my family after all these years. The truth is that I suffered in silence many times when he had his jealous moods, and sometimes he could become quite toxic, to the point that if we went out to enjoy a concert, I was not allowed to dance because, according to him, I was attracting other people's attention. He would end up creating a scene. It was not easy to break my chains, mainly because he would not show others the inappropriate behaviours he would have while being Mr Controlling with me. Eventually, I created courage and broke up. I had to deal with threatening calls like ' if you are not mine, you will not be of anyone else's,' and no one in my family believed me. Eventually, he understood that love and respect were not mutual and decided to love me from afar. He even got to meet my family after I got married.

I enjoyed the single life, had other relationships that lasted a few years, and then I got single again for five years when my whole life changed completely.

I had a successful career, money, close friends, and a loving family, all of which I'm proud of, but I longed for someone deserving of my love. Only when we see the big picture do we truly understand the reasons.

I met my soulmate less than three months after his first wife (my boy's birth Mum) passed away in March 2008. When we met in person, it felt like an amazing and exciting honeymoon, an experience we never had again after getting married. Everything was perfect as we traveled to incredible destinations, spent time with my best friends, and he met my entire family. A month later, after an over eleven-hour flight, I woke up in England, embracing my soulmate's family with unconditional love and strength. I transitioned from a successful career-driven person to suddenly becoming a mom and partner, living together right away. Sometimes, you must trust the universe's amazing and sometimes painful way of introducing turning points into our lives. I love my Mum for teaching me that a mother is the one who raises us. I've raised my two teenage sons with love and dedication since they were toddlers, and I'm grateful for the love that binds us.

In our over twelve-year relationship, our soulmate story, though unusual, encountered challenges that made us stronger. Like most couples, we faced moments when giving up seemed tempting, but we never did. Through our spiritual journey, we realized we were confronting past challenges and learned to accept and love each other unconditionally. Our love endures in various forms, as our souls stay connected, bringing peace despite his physical absence. One day, I'll share our story in a book, and who knows, it might become a movie. Everything is possible.

When my soulmate suddenly and unexpectedly transitioned to the spirit world, leaving me in a deep pit of sorrow and grief that almost consumed me whole, the knowledge that I did not serve any purpose because I completely lost connection with myself, my inner and external world. A huge sense of powerlessness consumed me. From my own experience, I can say that knowledge is only power when we choose to act and make the most of our wisdom through self-empowerment. No one was able to empower me while I was disconnected from life. I had to make the conscious decision to deal with grief and take small steps into the healing journey to reconnect and empower myself.

My faith, my love for my kids, and the healing from my late husband and my spiritual team were the fuel that kept me going. The love I received from my boys and so many people who know me worldwide touched my heart.

I heard many say to me similar things like 'You are the strongest and most determined person I know. I may not know your pain, but I know if there is someone who can overcome this situation, it's you.' or 'You have done so much for so many, and this is probably one of the times when others can give you some of the love and healing back that you always shared with others, so please accept our support.'

My previous experience with grief was when my grandfather passed away, and it was a peaceful one. However, the truth is, grief is not always about a specific event but rather about the change that we did not want to happen. It can be the loss of a person, a job, a relationship, or anything that we were attached to and had to let go of. Grief is a natural and normal human response to loss and can manifest in various ways, such as sadness, anger, confusion, and loneliness..

Healing from trauma involves recognizing and managing its impact. Trauma can take many different forms, such as the failure to meet basic human needs, physical or emotional abuse, natural disasters, or other life-altering events. It can cause profound changes in our lives and often leads to grief because it forces us to confront loss and change in a profound way. Even if the traumatic experience itself does not involve loss, the aftermath can create a sense of grief because we are left to process the changes that have occurred. Therefore, grief and trauma are often intertwined, and it's essential to acknowledge and address both in order to heal and move forward.

Other factors and nuances can impact the healing process, such as mental health conditions or physical health issues, the severity and duration of trauma or loss, an individual's personality, social support network, access to resources like therapy or medical care, and cultural and spiritual beliefs.

The most effective approach to healing may vary depending on the individual and nature of their experience. For example, Talk therapy may be more beneficial for some, while others may benefit more from physical exercise or mindfulness practices. Therefore, a personalized approach may be needed to address individual different needs. To promote healing, we need to develop qualities like patience, resilience, openness to new perspectives, and a willingness to confront difficult emotions. It's also essential to prioritize self-care, set healthy boundaries, show kindness and compassion to ourselves, seek support from others when needed, practice acceptance and forgiveness, engage in creative self-expression, and recognize that healing takes time and a willingness to work through challenging experiences.

In my case, I had to learn how to face and process the new reality that my children and I were experiencing. Even though I'm an evidential spiritual medium, I struggled to cope with the unexpected and unfair challenges we were facing at the beginning. But I don't feel ashamed to admit that. I knew I had to find ways to reconnect with my inner power and strength to overcome the trauma, grief, and uncertainty that were taking a toll on me. Despite feeling adrift and without my supportive family roots nearby, I had to find ways to reconnect with my inner power and to tap into my resilience, inner wisdom and courage.

As I began my journey of reawakening and healing from the inside out, I started to gain clarity. I realized that, before I could once again embrace my purpose with honesty and integrity and fully serve others in their healing journey, I needed to confront my own emotional limitations, pain, and insecurities. My heart had to be filled with enough love to remember my 'why,' my purpose, and my passion for helping people heal, connect with their inner world, and develop their personal and spiritual paths.

I went through a process of self-care, self-love, self-discovery, and self-intimacy to aid my identity quest. This process helped me reconnect with my soul, rediscover old and new passions, and establish a routine that felt fulfilling. Through this journey, my life experiences, and my skills in personal and spiritual development, I delved deep within myself, reconnecting with my inner wisdom and falling in love with myself once more. This reawakened my zest for life, inner peace, and personal power.

As part of my journey of growth and self-discovery, I boldly decided to invest in myself and work with a doctor and sex coach who supported me on my healing journey. I was able to connect with my inner self as a woman and rediscover my true passions and desires. Additionally, I was inspired by another amazing doctor who I could relate my experience and felt that we shared a similar story and mission. With determination and dedication, I accomplished my assignments and exams, and I am a proud certified Relationship, Intimacy and Love Coach, as well as an International certified Sexologist. This journey with all my previous knowledge and experiences has empowered me to help others connect with their own inner selves and embrace their sexuality with confidence and joy.

I have no regrets. You are all benefiting from the results of my transformation through this book or my one-to-one sessions, where I support my clients as they unravel and heal what's holding them back, harness their inner power and strength, overcome obstacles, heal their hearts, find inner peace, ignite love, and gain selfempowerment. This newfound sense of happiness and confidence allows them to fall in love with themselves and transform their inner world, their lives, relationships, and intimacy. They can then realign with their life's purpose, manifest their desires, evolve, inspire, and create a better world for themselves and those who are part of their intimate lives.

Having the courage to look within and confront our past is a transformative journey that can lead to profound personal growth and healing. It's an act of self-compassion and empowerment, a decision to no longer be held hostage by our past experiences, but to instead embrace them as opportunities for growth. When we summon the bravery to explore our inner world, we begin a process of self-discovery that can unlock the doors to understanding our emotions, motivations, and fears. It's a journey towards self-acceptance, where we also learn to forgive ourselves and others, and in doing so, we free ourselves from the chains of resentment and pain. This inner work is not always easy, but it's a path to greater self-awareness, resilience, and ultimately, a life lived with greater authenticity and fulfillment. So, I encourage you to embark on this journey with an open heart and a curious mind, for within your inner world lies the power to heal, grow, and create a brighter future.

It is essential to have clarity in what we desire and seek in a relationship and whether we feel ready for it or not. The mind and heart should be at ease with each other. To gain self-knowledge, all we need to do is look within ourselves by turning our attention inward and listening to our inner voice. Practice self-reflection, journaling, introspection, and self-analysis, and embrace your intuition while trusting your gut feelings; these can provide valuable insights into your true nature.

Throughout your journey reading this book, you will encounter numerous tools and techniques that I have applied in my own journey of awakening, healing, and personal growth. My personal journey in the realms of personal and spiritual development began over fifteen years ago. However, it's important to note that none of these tools will be effective without the desire to embrace and commit to your own journey of self-empowerment. It all begins with intention and your willingness to take action.

True empowerment cannot be given to us by others, but rather it comes from within. This means that we have the power to transform our lives and achieve our goals if we are willing to do the work.

To become truly empowered, we must be willing to look within ourselves, confront our fears and limitations, and take responsibility for our lives. This requires a deep level of self-awareness and self-reflection, as well as a commitment to personal and spiritual growth and development.

When we are empowered from within, we are not working on a quick fix. We allow ourselves to be able to make conscious and unconscious healing choices that will bring changes in our lives that align with our true desires and aspirations; that's also part of the process of how I support others because I know that if we want lasting changes and not a short term one, it requires courage and commitment to push through the obstacles and challenges, revisit painful traumas that we may have experienced but when we empower ourselves and recognise that we are the only ones who can make conscious and unconscious changes that will bring us closer to create a life that truly reflects our deepest desires and aspirations, we allow permanent transformation to take place.

Choose to heal, accept, have self-compassion, respect, be kind to yourself, learn to forgive, and step into a life of inner peace, joy, and growth.

Embrace all aspects of who you are and your journey towards self-knowledge and self-empowerment, and trust yourself and your innate abilities.

Space for Self-Reflection

In what ways have I transformed as a person over the course of my life, and what events or experiences have contributed to this transformation?

Am I aware of any limiting beliefs or negative self-talk that may affect my ability to connect with myself and others on a deeper level?

What patterns do I see in my past relationships, both romantic and platonic, both positive and negative, and how have these patterns impacted my ability to connect with others today, and influenced my personal growth and development?

Do I have a strong sense of self-worth and self-love, and am I able to express it in my relationship?

Am I able to take responsibility for my own happiness and not depend on others to fulfill my needs? If not, what story have I been telling myself and others?

What specific steps can I take to transform the areas of my life that are not aligned with my personal values and goals, including my relationships, into ones that are more fulfilling and reflective of who I want to be?

Have I ever had 'the talk' with my parents about sex? If so, how do I feel about their approach? If not, how do I feel about the lack of conversation on this topic?

Reflect on your earliest memories of sexual education and past experiences, including your cultural, religious, or societal beliefs around sex and consider how they have shaped your personal beliefs and behaviours. Develop a clear understanding of how these beliefs have influenced you, and explore any conflicts between them and your beliefs, behaviours around sex and relationships related to your personal values and goals. This process of self-reflection can help you identify outdated beliefs and create a new narrative around sex that aligns with your authentic self. You can also challenge these beliefs by exploring new perspectives and seeking out alternative sources of information and education.

Exploring your personal motivations for having sex can be empowering and lead to a deeper understanding of your desires and needs. What drives you to engage in sexual activity? Is it to express love and intimacy, to experience pleasure and relaxation, to explore your sexuality and connect with your body, or perhaps for adventure and excitement? Take some time to reflect on what brings you fulfillment and satisfaction in your sexual experiences.

How can I create a more fulfilling and satisfying sexual life, where I feel confident and empowered to explore self-intimacy, express myself, and communicate my desires and needs with my partner in an open and honest way, and create a safe space where we can both express ourselves authentically without shame or taboo?

How can I cultivate a deeper understanding and connection with myself and others in all areas of my life, including relationships, career, and personal growth, while staying true to my personal values and goals, and ensure that I am constantly evolving and aligning with my authentic self?

How do I feel about my capacity to learn, reprogram my mind, and change my emotional, mental, and physical states? Can I imagine the impact of shifting from shame to self-compassion and realizing my own voice?

How do I perceive the importance of personal responsibility, self-awareness, and self-reflection in my journey towards becoming truly empowered? How crucial do I believe it is in embracing all aspects of myself and trusting my path of self-knowledge and self-empowerment? Do I recognize the need for a commitment to personal and spiritual growth and development?

I honour and love being aware
of my body, sensations, feeling
and thoughts. The awareness
gives me clarity about who I
am and what I want. This helps
me choose behaviours that align
with my values, silence the inner
critic, and make wise choices
when I have opportunities
to grow through overcoming
challenges or difficult moments.

CHAPTER 2

Embracing Vulnerability

Vulnerability is a superpower that allows us to forge deep and meaningful connections with others. It is the key that unlocks the door to true intimacy, empathy, and understanding.

Yes, vulnerability can be uncomfortable and even scary at times. It requires us to step outside our comfort zones and face our fears head-on. It may involve exposing ourselves to feelings of shame, embarrassment, or self-criticism. But it is only by embracing these uncomfortable emotions that we can truly connect with others and build the kind of relationships that bring joy and fulfillment to our lives.

Being vulnerable requires courage, a willingness to take responsibility for our own emotions, and a deep commitment to staying true to ourselves, our feelings, and our values. It means showing up with boldness and authenticity, even in the face of uncertainty or rejection.

Healthy vulnerability involves sharing personal information in a way that is honest, authentic, and respectful of boundaries. It involves being open about one's emotions, needs, and fears, but doing so in a way that is appropriate for the context and the level of intimacy in the relationship.

On the other hand, oversharing can involve disclosing too much personal information too soon or in a way that makes the other person uncomfortable or violates their boundaries. It can also involve sharing information that is inappropriate for the context or the level of intimacy in the relationship.

There is definitely a line that can be crossed when being vulnerable in a relationship. It's important to be mindful of the other person's boundaries, and to take cues from their reactions to ensure that you are not oversharing or making them uncomfortable so adjust your level of vulnerability accordingly.

When we close down to vulnerability, we are depriving the people closest to us by not allowing them to know us entirely we may experience feeling disconnected and superficial when we are defensive and hesitant to being vulnerable. We create barriers to protect ourselves when we are reliant and powerless. The painful thoughts or sometimes even past experiences of being wounded, rejected, abandoned, ignored, or not having our needs met can impact how safe we feel with others. It can be overwhelming and if we don't feel safe, our flight or fight response gets our bodies back to safety by fighting off a threat or flighting, running away from it so we end up shutting ourselves off to a potential of love, intimacy, connection, joy, closeness.

At first glance, fear of vulnerability and fear of intimacy may seem like interchangeable terms, but there are key differences between them that are important to understand. While both involve feelings of fear and a desire to protect oneself, they stem from different sources and manifest in distinct ways.

Fear of vulnerability refers to a fear of being emotionally exposed or being seen as weak or imperfect. This fear can manifest in a number of ways, including reluctance to share personal experiences, feelings, and thoughts with others. Those who fear vulnerability may worry that others will judge them negatively, reject them, or exploit their weaknesses. As a result, they may avoid situations or relationships that require emotional openness, or they may put up emotional walls to protect themselves.

The fear of vulnerability can be traced back to past experiences, such as childhood trauma or rejection, that have created a deep-seated fear of being hurt or exposed. It can also be the result of cultural or societal pressures that value emotional strength and independence over vulnerability and interdependence.

Fear of intimacy (which we will discuss in more in depth in the next chapter) on the other hand, is a fear of emotional connection and dependence on others. This fear often manifests as a fear of abandonment or rejection, and those who fear intimacy may struggle to form deep, meaningful connections with others. They may avoid close relationships, or they may sabotage them by creating distance, picking fights, or engaging in other behaviours that push others away.

While fear of vulnerability and fear of intimacy often have different roots, they share some commonalities. Both involve a fear of being hurt or rejected, and both can be deeply ingrained and difficult to overcome. Additionally, both fears can have a negative impact on relationships, as they can make it difficult to form close, meaningful connections with others.

It's also worth noting that fear of vulnerability and fear of intimacy can be interconnected. For example, someone who is afraid of being vulnerable may struggle to form close relationships because they are afraid of being hurt or exposed. Alternatively, someone who is afraid of intimacy may avoid vulnerability because they fear being abandoned or rejected. It's possible for these fears to feed into one another, creating a cycle of avoidance and distance that is difficult to break.

Investing time and energy into being genuine is a valuable and worthwhile pursuit. When we are authentic and honest with ourselves and others, we create an environment of trust and openness. This allows for deeper connections and relationships to form, as we can truly connect with others on a meaningful level.

However, when we close ourselves off to one thing, we risk closing ourselves off to everything. If we are not willing to be vulnerable and share our true selves with others, we limit our ability to experience new things and expand our horizons. We may miss out on opportunities for growth, learning, and connection.

In our relationships with others, vulnerability is also crucial. Treating others as we would like to be treated requires us to be open and honest with them, even if it means being vulnerable. In a relationship with a partner, it is important to establish equality and mutual respect. This requires us to be vulnerable, to let go of our ego and see our partner as an equal and in that equality, we are able to build mutual respect for each other.

When equality is missing and there is an imbalance in a relationship, it is important to work together to establish an effective form of communication so we can improve our connection and the level of intimacy. Remember that, once upon a time, you both felt attracted to each other's values and had certain compatibilities that united you as a couple. Try to listen to each other's expectations and find ways to reconnect that flame that you both felt before. Allow your heart to remind you why you chose to be in a relationship with each other, avoid comparisons and external influence, and listen to each other from a place of empathy and compassion.

Only you two know what really happens or not within your relationship, inside your home, inside of your bedroom. But only you know what happens inside your own inner world. I do not encourage anyone to try mind reading in any relationship. I'm sure you can think of many situations where you have overthought something—we all do! It is part of being human. What makes the difference is developing the awareness to recognize a thinking error and choose to apply mindfulness for the best outcome.

It is also important to consider that, although in this book we are focusing on the importance of knowing yourself and feeling confident to embrace your vulnerability and sexuality, you are the only one that can know, feel and/or decide if there is any benefit in being vulnerable.

Ask yourself, what is the purpose? What is the cost of being vulnerable or not with this person or situation?

It is essential to weigh the potential benefits and costs of vulnerability before deciding to open up to someone. This involves reflecting on one's own values, needs, and goals, as well as considering the other person or situation involved.

Ultimately, the decision to be vulnerable should be based on what feels right and authentic for the individual. No one else can truly know how a person feels or what they need in each given situation, so it is important to listen to one's own inner voice and make a conscious and deliberate choice about whether to embrace vulnerability or not.

When deciding whom to trust and whom to be vulnerable with, it can be helpful to pay attention to red flags, such as manipulative behaviour, lack of empathy or a tendency to put their own needs above others. It is also important to trust your gut instincts and not ignore any feelings of discomfort or unease.

Ultimately, choosing whom to be vulnerable with is a personal decision that should be based on trust, safety and intuition. By being mindful and selective about whom we choose to share our vulnerabilities with, we can protect ourselves from potential harm while still cultivating deep, meaningful connections with those who deserve our trust and vulnerability.

I have experienced criticism, hurt, pain, betrayal of trust, and shame from narcissistic individuals, just as many of my clients have. These relatable experiences not only make us stronger but also help us grow and recognize the significance of establishing boundaries and, if necessary, distancing ourselves from toxic individuals who may project their fears and insecurities onto us. If you find yourself in any form of abusive relationship, I strongly encourage you to seek emotional support from a qualified professional.

There has to be mutual respect between the people involved in the relationship in order for there to be feelings of understanding and the ability to feel comfortable enough to be your authentic selves.

Independent of our relationship status, when we feel safe, we allow ourselves to open to new empowering experiences:

- ✓ We accept ourselves and develop confidence.
- ✓ Stay true to ourselves no matter what.
- ✓ We feel and know that we are worthy of love.
- ✓ We improve our self-esteem, self-concept, and self-regulation.
- ✓ We can talk about mistakes made coming from a place of compassion and understanding that we are not them.
- ✓ Feel courageous and develop resilience.
- ✓ Allow ourselves and our partner to improve our communication and understand each other more.
- ✓ We feel stronger to deal with uncertainty, risks, and emotional exposure.

- ✓ Feel motivated to learn and grow.
- ✓ We can prioritise our needs and happiness.
- ✓ Connect to ourselves and others.
- ✓ We avoid repressing or suppressing our emotions and needs.
- ✓ We share our feelings and experiences with people who have earned the right to hear them.
- ✓ We feel confident to be open and vulnerable with our partner, knowing they won't use our weakness or whatever we may feel afraid to share against us.
- ✓ We experience closeness, physical, emotional, energetic, romance…
- ✓ We feel more in tune with our own energy and the energy of those around us over time.
- ✓ We experience letting someone see into us, and share our insecurities, secrets, our desires, our deepest fantasies and what makes us feel uncomfortable.
- ✓ We increase trust, and intimacy because when we feel those levels of safety and connection, we know our partner has our best interests at heart. We feel fully accepted and not judged by them.

It's common for individuals who have experienced trauma to feel hesitant or even fearful of being vulnerable in their relationships, as they may worry about being hurt again. It's important to recognize that fear is a natural response. Trauma can alter the brain's wiring and impact one's ability to regulate emotions and trust others. Acknowledging and validating these feelings can be the first step towards healing and moving forward; there is no set timeline for recovery however as you become healed and become resilient, you empower yourself to build healthy relationships.

If, for any reason, you don't feel safe, don't push yourself to be vulnerable before you feel ready. Remember to trust on your instincts, believe in your own worth and value. Recognize that you deserve love and connection, and that vulnerability is a natural and necessary part of human relationships. Be kind to yourself; let go of anger, resentment, and frustration. Open up to uncertainty and the possibility of being hurt again. This is a conscious act of forgiveness and self-care, freeing us from negative emotions.

Often, fear of vulnerability is rooted in negative beliefs about oneself or others, such as "I'm not good enough" or "others will reject me if I show my true self." If you find yourself struggling with negative beliefs, take a moment to challenge them. Remind yourself of times when vulnerability has led to positive outcomes or connections with others and look for evidence that contradicts your negative beliefs.

Become more aware of your emotions and limiting beliefs, identify patterns or triggers that may be affecting our ability to be vulnerable. Take time to check in with yourselves regularly, and noticing how you are feeling in different situations. Are you feeling scared, anxious, or overwhelmed? Are you feeling happy, content, or fulfilled?

Take action to challenge your thoughts. When you shed those old, limiting beliefs, you will discover a new, stronger, and more resilient version of yourself. Change your state if you find yourself feeling negative emotions. One powerful technique is to change your physical state by standing up, moving around, or engaging in physical activity. This can help you shift your focus away and give you a burst of energy, and motivation to help you cultivate a more positive outlook and improve your emotional well-being. Being willing to discuss how you feel with others is an important element of establishing our bonds.

Take small acts of vulnerability; instead of avoiding discomfort, try to lean into it and explore what you can learn from it. You can start by expressing your feelings or needs to a trusted friend or family member.

If you are in a relationship, accept that we need someone else to lean on when we feel hurt, we require assistance from our loved ones to empathise with us and reciprocate in ways that strengthen our bonds. Be open and honest about your thoughts, desires, and feelings. When we share our fears with our loved ones that deeply cares for us and loves unconditionally, we develop a deeper level of intimacy, safety, trust and it's a way to grow together.

Address your partner in the eyes, hearing to what they have to say, and be able to devote time and concentration to the present moment.

Apply reflective listening, seek to understand the concept or idea that others are presenting to us. Don't just listen. Make yourself present and repeat the ideas back for understanding and confirmation.

There is no need to be overly exposed. You can choose to gradually build up to more intimate forms of vulnerability as you feel comfortable. Learn coping strategies that suits you in managing difficult feelings and acknowledge and celebrate your progress along the way.

Most of the times we can be too hard on ourselves and focus on what we have not done or achieved, embrace imperfections and flaws, we all have been there and we know its normal to have ups and downs in life, consider having a professional support or supportive and non- judgmental group can help us with validation and encouragement along the way, we can practice with them to reframe our experiences and identifying new ways of being vulnerable that feel authentic and empowering in a safe and controlled way.

Live your life by your values. When we live our life with integrity and are honest with our values, it can feel like all we manifest is in alignment. We feel confident in embracing vulnerability while having a sense of authenticity, belonging and maturity.

I know that is remarkable how scary is to leave the safety of your comfort zone. I have done a lot of healing and inner work to reclaim the power of my voice and created tools to improve my mental well-being to feel confident with who I am and be able to embrace vulnerability/ imperfections/ mistakes and rewrite my story in an empowered way, feeling confident to express myself and not be influenced by others' opinions.

Watch for red flags if you have people close to you who:

- Insults, patronises, yells, threatens and publicly humiliates others.
- Shows signs of negative jealousy or makes accusations.
- Blames you or others for everything that goes wrong.

- Deny things that are obvious or attempt to emotionally abuse or manipulate you.
- Like to tell people how they really feel or should feel.
- Project their frustrations and negative emotions onto you.
- Makes you, your opinions, and your needs feel less important than their ones.

No one deserves to have people in their life or relationships that verbally, emotionally, or physically abuse someone or even threaten them or make them feel isolated. As a consequence, it can create feelings of self-doubt, feeling a lack of control, and feeling not worthy of attention, low self-esteem, and an increased risk for depression, anxiety, loneliness, self-harm, and even suicidal thoughts.

If you ever feel unsafe or in a risky situation, seek support to navigate it confidently. Reach out to local domestic violence hotlines or specialized organizations for immediate assistance and safety planning. Consider professional counseling or therapy services, like sex therapy or trauma-informed care, where you can explore your feelings and develop effective communication strategies. Additionally, sexual health clinics and organizations supporting survivors of sexual violence can be valuable resources. Look for local or national organizations offering workshops, support groups, and educational materials on healthy relationships and sexuality. These resources empower you to navigate vulnerability with confidence and awareness.

Remember, it's always important to prioritize your safety and well-being. If you feel afraid or unsure, don't hesitate to reach out for help. The most important thing is to take steps towards getting the support and care that you need. Choose to inspire and motivate people, avoid giving your opinion, and influence those who have not asked for it, when we mind our own business, and focus on identifying and improving our own flawless, we also are giving focus to the number one person we should love unconditionally before being able to truly love and have compassion for others.

This person is the one you see in the mirror, it's you.

It takes courage to choose vulnerability over fear and find the confidence to show up as our true selves and from a place of growth and contribution. No one like to have to deal with uncertainty and what is unfamiliar to us and how uncomfortable we may become when we are exposed. Many of us are terrified of closeness, even if we aren't aware of it. Both closeness and vulnerability force us to let go of an old, comfortable identity and create a new one.

We are on this journey to create meaningful connections, building relationships that sustain us through the ups and downs of life, take risks, to trust that the people around us will accept us for who we are, build resilience towards rejection and criticism, and acknowledge that when people reject or are being judgmental to someone, they are only rejecting or criticizing a part of themselves that they are incapable to love, accept and make peace with. We accept them for who they are, we show them compassion and understanding, introduce healthy boundaries or let them go. That's when we know that we are growing in self-awareness, acceptance, love, respect, and maturity. We know our worthiness and we are allowing transformation to happen.

If you ever find yourself feeling powerless, it's crucial to remind yourself that nobody else holds power over you. You are the one in control of your own life and decisions. We all have moments when we question our abilities, but it's important to recognize that you are doing your best with the knowledge and resources available to you. Embrace the fact that you have the capacity to learn, grow, and overcome challenges, no matter how insurmountable they may seem. This acknowledgment can be a source of strength and motivation during difficult times, reminding you that you possess the inner resilience to face adversity and emerge stronger on the other side.

Take charge of your inner world; you hold greatness within you and deserve to be surrounded by those you choose to give and receive love from.

Be you, be brave, be love. Trust yourself and the universe through moments of discomfort. Vulnerability fosters connections based on trust, compassion, and understanding, leading to a profound sense of being seen and heard.

What is my personal definition of vulnerability, and how does it relate to my experiences and beliefs about trust, safety, and authenticity in my relationships?

How do I approach the process of self-discovery and self-awareness in the context of vulnerability and intimacy with others?

How do I define healthy vulnerability and distinguish it from oversharing? Am I mindful of the other person's boundaries and reactions when sharing personal information? How can I strike a balance between openness and respecting the appropriate level of intimacy in different relationships?

When it comes to choosing whom to trust and be vulnerable with, do I pay attention to red flags, such as manipulative behavior or a lack of empathy? How do I trust my instincts and honor any feelings of discomfort or unease? How can I create a safe and trusting environment for vulnerability in my relationships?

How have my experiences of closing myself off to vulnerability impacted my relationships, leading to feelings of disconnection and superficiality? In contrast, have I encountered transformative moments of vulnerability that have taught me valuable lessons about myself, the other person, and the barriers that hinder love, intimacy, and joy?

How do I understand the importance of authenticity and honesty in creating an environment of trust and openness in my relationships? Am I willing to invest time and energy into being genuine, even if it means stepping into vulnerability? How can I balance being authentic with protecting my own emotional well-being?

How do I handle conflicts or disagreements in relationships, especially when vulnerability is involved?

How do I integrate vulnerability and intimacy into my daily life, beyond just romantic relationships? How do I connect with others in a meaningful way while still maintaining my sense of self?

If I have experienced criticism, hurt, or shame from past relationships, how can I use those experiences to grow stronger and establish healthier boundaries? How can I recognize and remove toxic individuals from my circle of closeness to create a safer space for vulnerability? When necessary, am I willing to seek emotional support from qualified professionals?

How can I practice mindfulness and actively listen to my inner voice when deciding whom to trust and be vulnerable with? Am I aware of my own boundaries and needs, and do I prioritize my emotional well-being in these decisions? How can I cultivate trust and vulnerability in relationships with those who have earned it?

I am releasing the past and embracing a life of confidence and sexual empowerment, cherishing, and accepting every aspect of myself. Through this self-love, I am becoming more desirable and attractive, radiating a confidence and strength that allows me to be an incredible lover, full of passion and creativity. With each new experience, I am discovering new levels of ecstasy and fulfillment, embracing my true self, and living a life of joy and intimacy. My vulnerability is a beautiful part of my inner power, and I am grateful for all that I am and all that I will become.

CHAPTER 3

Empowering Yourself Through Healthy Boundaries

Boundaries are your personal guide to how you want to be treated, communicate and interact with others. They create a positive and respectful environment that leads to greater stability, understanding, and satisfaction. They are crucial for vulnerable individuals, as they establish a sense of safety and security in their lives.

Without healthy boundaries, we leave ourselves vulnerable to the harm of others. This can lead to feelings of helplessness, fear, and confusion and can further worsen the impact of past traumatic experiences. It's time to reclaim your power, you have the right to protect yourself and your well-being.

By learning to confidently say 'no,' you create more space for the things that matter most to you. Saying 'no' is not selfish; it's an act of self-care, self-love, and self-respect. Don't let others guilt or pressure you into saying 'yes' to things that do not align with your values or needs. Stand up for yourself and make your priorities a priority.

You are a unique and valuable person who deserves to be treated with respect and consideration. It's important to honour your own needs and desires, and to communicate them with confidence and assertiveness. Remember that you have the power to create positive and fulfilling relationships that bring joy and meaning into your life. Believe in yourself and trust in your ability to create the life you deserve.

Our personal values and expectations guide us in how we want to be treated in our relationships and interactions with others. By expressing and honouring these values, we create a positive and respectful environment that leads to greater stability, understanding, and satisfaction. Especially for those who are vulnerable, creating a safe and secure environment is crucial. We can empower ourselves by advocating for our needs and establishing trust in our relationships, leading to a more fulfilling and meaningful life.

When we allow others to cross our personal values and harm us in various ways, we can become vulnerable and experience feelings of helplessness, fear, and confusion. This can exacerbate the impact of past traumatic experiences, making it even more challenging to create a safe and secure environment.

It's natural to feel anxious or uncomfortable when setting new expectations or advocating for our needs. But it's important to remember that we are worthy of respect and consideration. We all deserve to have our own needs and desires met, and it's okay to express them. By developing assertive communication skills, we can express ourselves in a firm yet respectful way, building positive relationships and establishing trust. We can learn to manage difficult emotions and maintain our confidence, and take a step towards a happier and more fulfilling life.

What did you learn about relationship boundaries from past experiences?

It's important to be aware of these influences as they can also influence our beliefs about setting boundaries. For example, if someone grew up in a household where setting boundaries was not encouraged or respected, they may struggle to believe that setting boundaries is important or that they are entitled to do so. Alternatively, someone who has experienced positive relationships with healthy boundaries may be more likely to see the benefits of setting boundaries and may have a more positive outlook on their ability to do so.

Setting boundaries is a way of expressing and upholding our principles, preventing them from being compromised or violated. Past boundary violations can make it challenging for individuals to establish healthy boundaries. Without clear values and boundaries, relationships can lead to frustration, disappointment, resentment, and a sense of violation, potentially diluting our identities.

Have you ever felt like your boundaries were too weak, leaving you feeling vulnerable and struggling to express your true self?

Weak boundaries can create a sense of vulnerability and disconnect. They may lead to a feeling of being misunderstood, making it challenging to express our thoughts, needs, and desires honestly. This can result in decision-making difficulties and feelings of guilt, as well as a sense that our boundaries are not respected.

We also need to understand that when our boundaries are too rigid, they can impact our own rules, affect our ability to be good listeners and communicators, and hinder our capacity to empathize with others and address their problems. This can lead to superficial relationships. On the other hand, the establishment of personal boundaries contributes to a sense of security, stability, and order. These boundaries develop over time through various conclusions, assumptions, notions, views, attitudes, prior experiences, and social learning.

Being aware and clear about our boundaries, and developing assertive communication and distress tolerance skills (the ability to handle difficult emotions without feeling overwhelmed), are important personal assets that can help individuals maintain healthy boundaries. This, in turn, increases their confidence, safety, and ability to connect with themselves and others on a deeper level.

Below, you'll find different types of boundaries, along with healthy examples of what they might sound like:

Physical

We have them to protect our physical and emotional well-being by managing our physical space, touch, and proximity in different situations, while promoting mutual respect, safety, and healthy relationships.

"I choose to keep my demonstrations of affection private and reserved for specific times and places where I feel comfortable."

"My personal space and privacy are important to me, so please respect my boundaries by knocking and asking before entering my room."

"I have the right to decide who can touch me and when, so please don't touch me without my consent."

"I prefer not to engage in physical greetings like hugs or handshakes, as it's important for me to maintain my personal space and boundaries."

"Tickling can make me feel uncomfortable and disrespected, so please don't tickle me."

"I need my personal space when I'm working to stay focused, so please avoid standing too close to me during these times."

Environmental

Are set to create a safe and supportive space that promotes personal growth and emotional well-being by managing exposure to environmental stressors and cultivating a positive and empowering environment.

"I choose to use reusable alternatives instead of plastic or disposable products to reduce our impact on the environment."

"I thrive in a tidy and clutter-free living space, and I'm committed to maintaining it that way."

"I honour my need for quiet time in the morning to meditate and start my day on the right foot. Let's find a way to make it work for both of us."

"I feel most productive and energized when I have natural light in my workspace, so I prioritize it as a non-negotiable need."

"I prioritize creating a peaceful and relaxing home environment for both of us, where we can recharge and feel at ease."

"I value my focus and concentration when I'm working on a project, and I kindly ask for your support in respecting my boundaries by avoiding loud noises and interruptions."

Financial / material

Are the physical limitations we set to protect our personal space, belongings, and resources from being misused or taken advantage of by others.

"I have a savings goal that I'm working towards, so I need to limit my spending in certain areas."

"I have some financial goals I want to achieve, so I'd like to have some control over my own finances and not feel pressured to contribute to shared expenses."

"I won't be able to donate money to your cause this year, but I can donate my time by volunteering."

"I'm not comfortable with the idea of loaning out my clothes, but I can recommend some stores where you can find something similar."

"I need to stick to my budget, so I can't go out for an expensive dinner with you, but I'd love to cook a meal together at home."

"I won't allow others to take advantage of my generosity or willingness to share, I also need to prioritize my own financial stability."

Sexual

Are the rules we establish to protect our physical, emotional, and sexual well-being in sexual relationships, and to promote mutual respect, consent, and healthy communication around sexual desires and preferences.

"I understand that sexual activity can be a vulnerable experience, and I will only engage in it when I feel fully comfortable and ready."

"I honour on my own sexual boundaries and desires and will not compromise them for anyone else's expectations or desires."

"I need to build a strong emotional connection with my partner before exploring any sexual activity, and I need them to respect my pace and boundaries."

"I need to feel comfortable discussing my sexual history and any concerns around sexual health with my partner."

"I am allowed to change my mind about consent and sexual activity at any time and for any reason."

Emotional

Are set to protect our emotional well-being and promote healthy relationships, by managing our emotional responses to different situations, communicating our needs and limits effectively, and avoiding emotional harm and abuse.

"My emotions and reactions are my own responsibility, and I can't be held accountable for anyone else's."

"I value myself and my own needs, and I need you to respect my boundaries and trust my judgement."

"I'm here for you, but I also need to take care of myself. Please understand that I may need some space to process my own feelings before I can offer support."

"I appreciate your input, but I need to make my own decisions. Please respect my choices even if they're different from yours, as I believe in my ability to choose what's best for me."

"Our relationship is important to me, and I want us both to have equal say in it. I hope you can consider my needs and feelings as well as your own."

"I feel hurt when you yell at me, and I believe we can communicate better. Let's listen to each other calmly and respectfully, so we can work through our issues together."

Time

Are the limits we set for ourselves regarding how we allocate and use our time, in order to protect our personal and emotional well-being, establish healthy relationships, and achieve our goals.

"I value our time together, but I also need time to pursue my own interests and hobbies outside of our relationship and have my own individuality."

"I'm not able to respond to work emails outside of work hours, as I need to prioritize my personal time and self-care."

"I value my time and do not tolerate lateness. If we have a meeting or appointment scheduled, I expect us to be on time."

"It's important for my mental and emotional well-being to practice self-care and have alone time to recharge every day, so I won't be available for phone calls or texts after 8 pm."

"I want to spend more quality time with my family, so I'm limiting evening commitments during the week."

"I value clear communication and concrete plans. If plans aren't made by Friday, I'll take responsibility for making other arrangements."

Expectations

Are used to manage our own and others' expectations.

"I recognize the importance of self-care and mental health, and I expect my partner to prioritize their own well-being as well. I also believe in supporting each other's self-care practices and creating a healthy balance in our relationship."

"I need you to respect my values and beliefs, even if they are different from yours. I expect that we can have a healthy and respectful discussion about our differences."

"I prioritize respect and kindness in my relationships, and I expect my partner to treat me with the same level of care and consideration they would give to themselves."

"I value my independence and my ability to make my own decisions, and I expect my partner to respect my autonomy. At the same time, I commit to working collaboratively with my partner to make joint decisions that support our mutual goals and values."

"I need to be with someone who respects my boundaries and is willing to compromise. I expect that we can work together to find a mutually beneficial solution when our needs and wants are different."

"I value my personal space and time with my friends and family. I expect that we can both have our own social lives and not be overly dependent on each other for our happiness."

Relationships

Are rules that we use to establish our interactions with others to promote mutual respect, emotional safety, and healthy communication while protecting our own autonomy and well-being.

"I expect that we can both take responsibility for our own emotions and not blame each other for how we feel."

"I value privacy and respect in relationships, and I don't feel comfortable discussing certain aspects of my past."

"I appreciate a relationship that values equality and mutual support, where we can both contribute equally and help each other reach our goals."

"I prioritize relationships where we can both be open and vulnerable without fear of judgment or criticism."

"I'm not comfortable with being in a relationship where one person is overly controlling. I expect that we can both have a say in decision-making and respect each other's autonomy."

"I'm not comfortable with being pressured into doing things I'm not ready for. I expect that we can both respect each other's boundaries and not push each other beyond our comfort zones."

Non- Negotiable

Are rules that we establish to protect our fundamental needs, values, and beliefs, and are essential for their emotional and psychological well-being, personal growth, and self-respect.

"I choose to prioritize my self-respect and dignity. I will only allow myself to be treated with respect and kindness, and I will not compromise on this boundary."

"I value my cultural and religious identity, and it's important to me to be with someone who respects and values that. This is a non-negotiable boundary for me."

"I prioritize my safety and comfort, and I will not tolerate anyone who doesn't respect my sexual boundaries and preferences. This is a non-negotiable boundary for me."

"I make choices that align with my personal values and beliefs around substance use, and it's important to me to have a partner who respects and supports those choices. This is a non-negotiable boundary for me."

"I prioritize my emotional well-being and the health of my relationships, and it's important to me to be with someone who is willing to compromise and make an effort to build a strong connection with me. This is a non-negotiable boundary for me."

"I choose to keep the details of my intimate life private and respect the privacy of my partner. This is a non-negotiable boundary for me."

Digital

Are the guidelines we establish for our use of technology and online communication to protect our privacy, managing our time and energy, promoting healthy relationships, and maintaining our well-being in the digital world.

"I choose to prioritize face-to-face communication and connection over constant phone use, so I'll be putting my phone away during our meal."

"I value my time and productivity, and I need to focus on my work/studies without digital distractions. I won't be responding to messages or notifications until my designated break time."

"I respect my privacy and want to maintain control over my personal information, so please ask me before sharing any of my details."

"I am committed to maintaining a positive online presence and want to avoid negativity, drama, or unwanted attention. Please do not post any pictures of me or us without my permission."

"I prioritize good sleep hygiene and want to avoid the temptation to use my phone before bedtime, so I won't be using my phone in the bedroom at night."

"I value our relationship and want to keep certain aspects private, so I won't be sharing intimate details or photos on social media. Let's keep our relationship just between us."

Spiritual

Are set to protect our personal beliefs, values, and practices from being disrespected or disregarded by others, while also respecting the spiritual beliefs of others.

"I prioritize self-care and take time every day to connect with my inner self through meditation and reflection."

"I am open-minded and willing to learn from others, but I don't compromise my own values and beliefs to please others."

"I set clear boundaries with others to protect my energy and prevent negative influences from affecting my spiritual well-being."

"I don't engage in gossip or negative talk because I believe in the power of positive energy and its ability to uplift and inspire."

"I respect and honour all spiritual beliefs and practices, but I have chosen a different path for myself. I will not engage in discussions or activities that conflict with my spiritual values and beliefs. I will also not tolerate anyone disrespecting my spiritual choices or attempting to impose their beliefs on me."

"I trust my intuition and make decisions based on my inner guidance rather than external pressures or expectations."

Social

Are established to protect our personal space, time, and emotional well-being in social situations, while also promoting respect, inclusion, and healthy communication with others.

"I value my alone time and make sure to schedule it regularly. I respect my need for space and communicate it clearly to others."

"I surround myself with people who support and uplift me, and I am not afraid to distance myself from those who do not."

"I am confident in setting boundaries and assertively communicate them when necessary. I prioritize my own well-being above pleasing others."

"I make intentional choices about how I spend my time and with whom. I feel empowered to decline social invitations that do not align with my priorities."

"I trust my own judgment and intuition about what social activities feel comfortable and enjoyable for me. I do not let others pressure me into anything that doesn't feel right."

"I am selective about what personal information I share with others and am not obligated to disclose anything I don't feel comfortable with."

"I am true to myself and my values, even in social situations where others may have different opinions or beliefs. I stay authentic and stand up for what I believe in."

Although it may be difficult, it's important to prioritize your own needs and desires even if it means disappointing others. Don't let the fear of upsetting someone prevent you from living your best life. Remember, you have the right to feel safe and respected in your relationships.

It can be helpful to communicate with others when setting boundaries. Explaining the reason behind your boundary can help others understand and respect your needs. It's okay if they don't like it or get offended, because you deserve to prioritize yourself and your well-being. Having a strong sense of self-esteem can make it easier to stand your ground and say "no" when you need to.

Sometimes, when we set boundaries, it might lead to misunderstandings or reactions from others. It's essential to remember that each person has their perspective shaped by their own experiences. They might not fully understand your intentions, just as you might not fully understand theirs. It's an opportunity for both parties to reflect on their feelings and responses.

Consider why setting boundaries feels necessary for you. What are your needs and desires in your relationships? How do these boundaries align with your values and well-being? Likewise, try to understand why others might react the way they do. What are their fears or concerns? What experiences might be shaping their responses?

It's important to note that reactions such as 'narcissism,' 'manipulative behavior,' and 'victim mentality' are sometimes associated with individuals who might resist or react negatively when someone sets healthy boundaries. However, it's not about judging or labeling behaviors but gaining insight into the complexity of human interactions.

By seeking to understand and educate ourselves about these behaviors, we create space for empathy and open communication, fostering healthier relationships for everyone involved. This process also allows each person to find their answers and grow together.

Effective communication while setting boundaries is vital. Practice assertive yet respectful communication skills to maintain positive relationships, even in uncomfortable moments. It's natural to feel uneasy, but you can manage it with coping strategies. Embracing healthy boundaries leads to self-empowerment and growth, even amid discomfort and misunderstandings.

What are your personal values and needs in a relationship? How do they align with your actions and decisions?

How effectively do you express and share your feelings and experiences with people who have earned the right to hear them?

Have you ever asked yourself if you truly know what you like and do not like in your relationship with yourself and others, and if you feel confident about your rules, expectations, and boundaries?

What did I learn about relationship boundaries from past experiences? What did I learn about asking for help and saying "No" to people?

How do I differentiate between healthy and unhealthy boundaries? What are some signs that indicate that my boundaries may need to be revaluated?

Are there any areas of my life where I struggle to set and maintain boundaries? What can I do to improve in these areas?

Have I ever experienced a situation where I set a boundary, but it was not respected? How did I react and handle the situation, and what did I learn from it?

How has my fear of saying "no" and setting boundaries contributed to feelings of guilt, resentment, or a lack of control in my relationships?

Have I noticed any negative consequences of having rigid boundaries, such as difficulties in listening, communicating, or developing deeper connections with others?

My boundaries reflect my self-respect and self-love, and I trust my intuition to set them according to my needs and values. I communicate my boundaries clearly and confidently, without feeling guilty or ashamed, and prioritize my well-being to create a safe space for myself to grow and thrive. Setting and enforcing my boundaries is an act of self-care and self-preservation that will lead me to a more fulfilling and authentic life. I am not responsible for others' emotions or reactions to my boundaries, and I deserve relationships that honour and respect them. I can adjust my boundaries to serve my values and needs and trust that doing so will lead to a happier and more fulfilling life.

CHAPTER 4

Awakening into Intimacy

I n a relationship, there are infinite possibilities for intimacy - each one a unique opportunity for growth, connection, and fulfillment. These layers of intimacy are like pieces of a puzzle, each one contributing to the beautiful picture that is your relationship. From the most superficial interactions to the deepest, most meaningful moments, intimacy offers a chance to learn, grow, and love.

Through emotional intimacy, we create a safe haven for vulnerability, sharing our deepest thoughts and feelings without fear of judgement. Intellectual intimacy invites us to explore new ideas and expand our horizons. Recreational intimacy is a chance to let loose and have fun with our partner, creating memories and shared experiences.

And that's just the beginning. Creative intimacy allows us to share our artistic passions with one another. Sexual intimacy is an opportunity to explore our deepest desires and connect with our partner on a physical level. Relational intimacy strengthens our bond by nurturing communication and trust. Conflict intimacy allows us to work through disagreements in a healthy, productive way. Crisis intimacy deepens our connection by weathering difficult times together. Experimental intimacy allows us to try new things and grow together. Experiential intimacy is a chance to create shared memories and adventures. Existential intimacy invites us to explore life's biggest questions together. Financial intimacy is a chance to work as a team to create a stable and prosperous future. Career intimacy supports us as we strive to achieve our professional goals. Parenting intimacy brings us closer as we work together to raise our children. Social intimacy allows us to explore the world together, meet new people and try new things. Family intimacy connects us with our loved ones and creates a sense of belonging. Transcendent intimacy is a chance to connect with something greater than us, whether it be spirituality, nature, or the universe.

Self-intimacy empowers us to recognize ourselves as we truly are, embrace our values, and acknowledge our self-worth. Be aware of your flaws, apply self-love, respect, and compassion, and trust your instincts. This is all part of an inner work that can sometimes bring insecurity and negative emotions. We need to investigate the root cause of these negative emotions with the best knowledge we have about the situation and the people involved. This gives you confidence that what once was is in the past, and whatever happens cannot hurt us anymore. It's a path we all should be proud of, regardless of whatever we may have had to overcome. Acknowledge the lessons learned so you feel able and empowered to move on.

When we allow ourselves to start the awakening journey into intimacy, it is important to never forget every single one of us has a story, and our experiences provide a unique opportunity to learn, heal, and grow. I welcome you to detach from the outcome and enjoy the journey.

When we prioritise trust, communication, vulnerability, emotional and physical connection and dedicate regular quality time to focus on our relationship, we are also giving ourselves permission to develop practices that will not only keep the spark alive and the connection fulfilling for a lifetime but will also create space for growing together to resolve conflict in a timely manner without creating emotional disconnection.

Self-intimacy is a powerful practice that can have numerous benefits for our mental, emotional, spiritual and physical health, cultivating a deep and meaningful connection with ourselves, taking the time to understand our thoughts, feelings, needs and desires, identify our values, beliefs, interests and passions and learning to be comfortable with it, breaking free from patterns of self-sabotage and negative self-talk and develop a strong sense of self-worth and confidence to the point that we are less likely to seek validation or approval from others. By understanding ourselves, we are able to improve our ability to cope with stress and difficult emotions. We are better equipped to handle challenges and setbacks, we are also more likely to seek help when we need it, as we are not afraid to acknowledge our vulnerabilities and seek support from others, we effectively empathize, recognize and relate to our and others emotions, improve our communication styles and establish healthier relationships leading to a more positive and empowered sense of self and developing a sense of purpose and meaning in life and work towards fulfilling it.

Advantages of Awaken to self-intimacy.

> Unlock your boundless creativity and ignite your imagination to new heights.

> Break free from self-sabotage and negative self-talk and unleash your full potential.

> Experience deeper self-compassion, self-love, respect, acceptance, and control over your emotions.

> Cultivate a meaningful and fulfilling relationship with yourself that brings joy and harmony to your life.

> Build self-worth and confidence.

> can bring immense joy, fulfillment, and self-discovery into our life. We learn to trust your intuition and make decisions with ease and grace.

> We become more connected to your true self, your passions, and your purpose in life. We learn to listen to your inner voice and trust your instincts, which can help you make better decisions and navigate life's challenges with more ease and grace. Helps us recognizing that we are a unique and valuable individual, worthy of love and respect.

> Helps us recognizing that we are a unique and valuable individual, worthy of love and respect.

> Allow us more easily connect with others in a genuine and authentic way, free from the fear of judgment or rejection.

> Build resilience to face life's challenges with grace and strength.

> Discover your unique sense of purpose and meaning, and let it guide you to greatness.

- ➢ Improves communication, empathy leading to meaningful connections.
- ➢ Learn to manage stress and difficult emotions with ease and grace.
- ➢ Develop empathy and compassion for yourself and others, and transform your relationships.
- ➢ Express your true self freely and boldly and unleash your full potential.
- ➢ Love and accept yourself unconditionally, and watch your life transform before your eyes.
- ➢ Understand your own emotions and those of others and connect on a deeper level.
- ➢ Live a life that aligns with your core values, beliefs, interests, and passions.
- ➢ Build inner strength and resilience and overcome any obstacle that comes your way.
- ➢ Create a life that is authentic, meaningful, and fulfilling, and live it with passion and purpose.
- ➢ Build a powerful sense of inner strength and self-reliance.

Disadvantages of neglecting self-intimacy.

Mental:

- ➢ Difficulty coping with challenges and setbacks.
- ➢ Difficulty coping with stress.
- ➢ Difficulty making decisions.
- ➢ Difficulty with authenticity and showing up as our true selves.
- ➢ Difficulty with forgiveness.
- ➢ Feeling stuck or stagnant in life.
- ➢ Inability to find meaning and purpose in life.
- ➢ Lack of focus and concentration.
- ➢ Lack of self-awareness, self-love, respect, regulation.
- ➢ Negative self-talk and self-criticism.
- ➢ Poor communication.

Emotional:

- ➢ Difficulty expressing emotions and needs effectively.
- ➢ Difficulty regulating emotions.
- ➢ Difficulty relaxing and experiencing physical pleasure.
- ➢ Difficulty setting boundaries and saying "no".
- ➢ Difficulty with self-love and seeking validation from others.
- ➢ Feeling blocked in creative pursuits.
- ➢ Increased sense of loneliness and isolation.
- ➢ Lack of gratitude.
- ➢ Lack of inner peace and stillness.
- ➢ Lack of joy and creativity.
- ➢ Low self-esteem and self-worth.
- ➢ Shame and guilt.
- ➢ Tendency to numb or avoid emotions through unhealthy coping mechanisms such as substance abuse, overeating, or self-harm.
- ➢ We may hold onto resentments or grudges, which can prevent us from experiencing inner peace and healing.

Spiritual:

- ➢ Difficulty experiencing a sense of connection to something greater than oneself.
- ➢ Difficulty finding a sense of inner peace and stillness.
- ➢ Difficulty connecting with one's intuition and inner wisdom.
- ➢ Difficulty experiencing a sense of transcendence or mystical experience.
- ➢ Difficulty engaging in practices such as meditation, yoga, or prayer.
- ➢ Difficulty experiencing a sense of awe and wonder in life.
- ➢ Difficulty connecting with a sense of gratitude and appreciation for life.
- ➢ Disconnection from inner wisdom.
- ➢ Disconnection from nature and the world around us.
- ➢ Disconnection from our passions and interests.
- ➢ Feeling disconnected from our spiritual community.

➢ Prevent us from connecting with our higher selves and experiencing a sense of inner peace and purpose.

➢ Inability to connect with higher consciousness and spiritual insights.

➢ Lack of connection with a higher power or sense of spirituality.

➢ Lack of connection with the divine.

➢ Inability to surrender and trust in the flow of life.

➢ Inability to connect with our deepest desires and manifest them in the world.

Physical Health:

➢ Difficulty maintaining healthy habits such as regular exercise and a balanced diet.

➢ Increased risk of chronic pain and tension due to stress and tension in the body.

➢ Increased risk of developing mental health disorders such as depression, anxiety disorders, and eating disorders.

➢ Increased risk of developing physical health problems such as heart disease, diabetes, and obesity due to unhealthy coping mechanisms such as overeating, smoking, or not getting enough sleep.

➢ Physical symptoms such as headaches, muscle tension, and fatigue.

➢ Sexual dysfunction.

Take time to explore your inner world, give yourself permission to discover the magic within you and watch as your relationships, career, and overall well-being begin to thrive.

Give yourself permission to awaken to self-intimacy and explore the depths of your being, embrace the principles of consent, seek the explicit and enthusiastic agreement of all parties involved, whether in a sexual context or in everyday interactions and create a foundation for healthier and more authentic relationships.

Consent can be withdrawn at any time and should respect our partner's decisions. Never assume that someone is comfortable with an activity, and always check-in and ask for their consent before engaging in any physical or sexual activity.

Asking for and giving consent, promotes a trusting and caring relationship where all parties involved in any physical, sexual, or emotional activity are comfortable and safe. It prevents coercion and abuse by ensuring that everyone involved is freely and willingly agreeing to participate.

We feel we can fully enjoy the experience without worrying about causing harm or discomfort. Consent can create a sense of mutual pleasure and connection, leading to exploring new experiences and pushing our own boundaries in a safe and respectful way.

Blocks to Intimacy

Blocks to intimacy can be rooted in various past experiences and unconscious beliefs. These experiences and beliefs can shape an individual's perception of themselves, others, and relationships, and can make it difficult to form close, meaningful connections.

For example, a person who has experienced trauma or abuse in the past may develop a fear of vulnerability and struggle with opening up to others. This fear can stem from the belief that being vulnerable puts them at risk of further harm and can lead to patterns of avoidance or emotional detachment in relationships.

Similarly, an individual who has grown up in an environment where they were not allowed to express their emotions may struggle with communicating their feelings in close relationships. They may have internalized the belief that emotions are a sign of weakness or that expressing them is not acceptable, and as a result, find it difficult to share their inner experiences with others.

Attachment styles play a critical role in shaping our experiences of intimacy and sexuality they are deeply rooted in early experiences with caregivers and shape how we perceive and relate to others, particularly in close relationships which can influence our expectations, attitudes, and behaviours in adult relationships.

Identifying and exploring attachment styles helps us to better understand our emotional patterns and behaviours in relationships and identify negative or limiting beliefs that may be contributing to their fear of intimacy and work towards developing more secure and meaningful connections with others. For example, an individual with an avoidant attachment style may have learned to avoid closeness and emotional connection in relationships to protect themselves from potential rejection or abandonment.

Understanding your own attachment style can help you better understand and address your fear of intimacy. It can also help you identify patterns in your relationships and work towards building more secure attachments as an exercise you can write down any experiences or memories from childhood that may have shaped the way the individual relates to others.

If we strive to develop a secure attachment style, we can approach our relationships with openness and vulnerability, knowing that we are worthy of love and support. By expressing our emotions and needs in healthy ways, we can build strong and lasting connections with those who share our values and priorities.

The four primary attachment styles are:

Secure attachment style: Individuals with a secure attachment style tend to feel comfortable with emotional and physical closeness in their relationships. They trust their partners and believe that they will be there for them when needed. Securely attached individuals feel safe and secure in their relationships and are able to communicate their needs and emotions effectively.

Anxious-preoccupied: Individuals with an anxious-preoccupied attachment style tend to crave closeness and intimacy, but may also feel insecure and worry about rejection. They often have negative views of themselves and fear abandonment or rejection from their partners. They may be clingy and seek reassurance from their partners to feel secure in the relationship.

Dismissive-avoidant: Individuals with a dismissive-avoidant attachment style tend to avoid emotional and physical closeness in their relationships. They may prefer to be alone and may feel uncomfortable with intimacy and vulnerability. They tend to be independent and self-sufficient, often feeling that they don't need others to feel fulfilled.

Fearful-avoidant: Individuals with a fearful-avoidant attachment style tend to experience conflicting desires for intimacy and independence. They may desire emotional closeness and connection but also fear rejection and abandonment. They may feel unworthy of love and struggle with self-doubt and anxiety in their relationships.

Individuals with secure attachment styles tend to have positive expectations of relationships and feel comfortable with emotional intimacy. They are able to trust others and rely on them for support, and they are comfortable expressing their own emotions and needs. These individuals tend to have satisfying, long-term relationships with partners who share their values and priorities.

On the other hand, individuals with insecure attachment styles may struggle with intimacy in different ways. Those with an anxious-preoccupied attachment style tend to crave intimacy and reassurance but may struggle with fears of abandonment and rejection. They may cling to their partners and become overly dependent, leading to relationship instability and conflict. Individuals with a dismissive-avoidant attachment style, on the other hand, tend to avoid intimacy altogether, often due to a fear of vulnerability and dependence. They may prioritize independence and self-reliance over emotional closeness, leading to difficulties forming and maintaining close relationships.

Other factors that can cause Intimacy blockages are:

Communication difficulties, such as a fear of conflict or difficulty expressing emotions, may cause individuals to avoid close relationships or struggle with emotional and physical closeness. Don't let the fear of expressing yourself hold you back from experiencing deep connections with others. Take the leap and open yourself up to the possibility of intimacy.

Communication difficulties/lack of skills are associated with our struggle to express emotions or confidently communicate our needs, desires, and boundaries, which leads to misunderstandings and conflicts, making it difficult to build trust and connection. Communication is a two-way street, and it's important to develop communication skills, practice active listening, empathy and assertiveness, be clear and concise and be open and receptive to feedback from others.

Cultural or religious factors may influence an individual's beliefs. For example, in some cultures or religions, marriage and commitment are highly valued, and individuals may feel pressure to marry or enter into long-term relationships. This pressure to commit may trigger a fear of intimacy, where the individual may feel overwhelmed or trapped by the idea of settling down and losing their freedom or independence.

Moreover, cultural, or religious beliefs about gender roles, sexuality, and relationships can also shape an individual's perceptions of intimacy. For example, some cultures or religions may view men as the initiators of sexual activity, and women as passive recipients. These beliefs can create a power imbalance in relationships, making it difficult for individuals to feel comfortable expressing their desires or boundaries. Your beliefs are important, but don't let them hold you back from experiencing the joys of intimacy. Embrace your unique cultural or religious perspective and explore the beauty of intimate relationships.

Fear of commitment or fear of being tied down or losing freedom or fear of loss of independence, this fear can be rooted in a variety of factors, such as a fear of missing out on other experiences or a fear of making the wrong choice. Some individuals may fear that forming close relationships will lead to a loss of independence or autonomy. It's important to maintain your independence but don't let the fear of losing it hold you back from experiencing the beauty of intimate relationships. Embrace freedom, and vulnerability and open yourself up to the possibility of deep connection.

Past rejection or abandonment and Inability to trust leads us to feel we need to protect ourselves from future hurt and end up avoiding close relationships or keeping people at a distance. Our past reminds us that we had been through situations that allowed us to grow without defining us. When we want to rebuild trust in intimacy it's important to create a safe and supportive environment where both parties involved feel heard, seen, and valued, taking the time to address underlying issues, being consistent in our behaviour, and being patient with the process while we open ourselves up to the possibility of connection and joy.

Sexual orientation or gender identity issues can affect individuals that may have difficulty with intimacy due to a fear of rejection or discrimination. With courage and determination, we can create a world that values diversity and celebrates the beauty of our differences, starting with us, embracing ourselves fully, with all our unique qualities and quirks the power of self-acceptance, self-love can give us.

Insecurity and self-doubt, as individuals may feel unworthy of love or may believe that others will eventually reject or abandon them. We all are worthy of love and connection, no matter our doubts or insecurities. Embrace your unique qualities and believe in your worthiness to live an authentic life.

Mental health or physical conditions, such as anxiety, depression, post-traumatic stress disorder (PTSD), sexual dysfunction or chronic pain, may make it difficult to engage in emotional and physical intimacy. Embrace your healing journey with love, acceptance, compassion, and an open heart to allow transformations to occur. Seek support, there are many amazing healers and professionals in this world. Explore creative ways to intimately connect with your body, mind, and soul.

Substance abuse or addiction can make it difficult to form close relationships, as individuals struggling with addiction may prioritize their substance use over their relationships. The fear of losing control or facing rejection due to their addiction can also contribute to a fear of intimacy. It takes great courage to seek help, whether through therapy, support groups, or other resources, and to embark on the journey towards recovery, healing, growth, and the reclamation of a new life filled with love, joy, and deep connections with oneself and others. This journey is truly worth taking.

Negative beliefs, low self-esteem, negative self-image, and self-talk are big blockages. When we believe that we are not good enough or that we are undeserving of love, we may struggle to open ourselves up to others and accept their love in return. You are deserving of love and affection, and with some self-reflection and positive self-talk, you can begin to break free from these limiting beliefs, no matter your perceived flaws or imperfections.

Embrace self-love and work towards accepting and celebrating all aspects of yourself.

When someone comes from a background of abuse or neglect, this person can develop emotional scars that are triggered if they feel like they are being verbally abused, cheated, neglected, threatened, or abandoned.

Some of the blockages to intimacy can be related to childhood trauma, poor self-image, an inability to communicate feelings or speak out, triggers from the past, anger, poor role modeling, false or negative beliefs, past sexual or physical abuse or neglect, brokenness from past relationships, excessive devotion to their job, children, home, career, and more!

When you are intimate with yourself, you become better equipped to establish intimacy with your partner in a relationship. Sex and intimacy are vital components of the emotional space within a relationship, in addition to their role in procreation and the other well-known health benefits of sex. Couples who report high levels of relationship satisfaction also tend to have healthy sex lives. So, don't hesitate to discuss it with your partner and take things slowly to ensure both of you are comfortable.

An intimate relationship is one in which both partners must be awake and authentic, address their concerns or fears, and grow in love. It involves being genuine, truthful, loyal, and loving toward each other.

Regarding the topic of a sex life, we often hear the terms 'making love' and 'having sex' used interchangeably, even though there is a distinction between the two. Both involve sex, but each carries a different level of emotional connection and closeness. The difference lies in the state of mind of the individuals involved.

Making love' is the art of connecting your minds and souls through sexual intercourse, while 'just sex' fulfills a basic biological need for most humans, allowing them to satisfy their physical desires and needs. Unlike 'just sex,' making love is not solely focused on achieving a physical goal. When two individuals make love, there is an emotional connection, a mental connection, and bodily harmony.

Making love allows us to experience the metaphysical state of oneness, and it is the purest kind of soul nourishment in which two individuals are spiritually and emotionally united. There is no lust in true love since we are not drawn to their physical looks. Love is essentially the union of two souls.

Sexual response involves more than simply becoming sexually excited; it requires dedicated personal attention over an extended period. Sometimes, you may not feel the same way every day, but it's important to stay connected to your body and listen to what it's telling you. It's also okay to say "no" if that's what you want.

Steps and ways that any individual can take to practice Intimacy.

- Believe in your own inner wisdom.
- Be grateful for every single moment and do not take each other for granted; give compliments and acknowledge each other's efforts; use achievements and even struggles as an opportunity to grow, even if you cannot see the lessons in it yet.
- Create a safe and nurturing environment for yourself: This can involve decluttering your space, lighting candles, or engaging in activities that bring you peace and comfort.
- Accept yourself in your current state.
- Give yourself the space to be yourself.
- Write a letter to your soul.
- Pay attention to your emotions.
- Learn about your inner critic.
- Let your loved one know when you would like to have a conversation that requires them to be fully present in the moment to truly listen.
- Experience freedom from wounds of trauma.
- No is No. Learn to say it with confidence!
- Be free of guilt/shame—this is a common issue I work with most of my clients on. You are not alone! Even I have had experience with it in the past. It does not define who we are. To have shame is to live a life

without a purpose. When we feel confident, we stop being the victim and start to accept that we are perfect, imperfect beings.

➢ Do mirror work, acknowledge your existence, give yourself compliments, and learn how to see yourself as a whole, not as the part you want to pick apart in the mirror.

➢ Be friends with yourself; be your best partner.

➢ Engage in self-reflection and self-care activities, such as journaling, meditating, or practicing self-compassion, can help individuals become more in touch with their needs.

➢ Pursuing personal growth and development, such as through therapy, personal development courses, or self-study, can help individuals become more in touch with their own emotions and needs, which can increase their capacity for intimacy.

➢ Engaging in physical touch: Physical touch is an important aspect of intimacy, and individuals can practice physical touch through activities such as self-massage, yoga, or simply hugging themselves.

➢ Trust yourself and be your own raving fan, your guru, your own influencer, and stop being a follower.

➢ Cultivating a gratitude practice, such as keeping a gratitude journal or expressing gratitude for positive experiences

➢ Create a safe and nurturing environment for yourself: This can involve decluttering your space, lighting candles, or engaging in activities that bring you peace and comfort.

➢ When you become more open to being your full and true self, you will feel free and safe. You will be happy and open, capable of being intimate with others. Manage your expectations and accept that trusting someone to do what they said they are going to do may take time and that's okay.

➢ Dissatisfaction in your intimate relationship leads to frustration, anger, hurt, guilt, cynicism, insecurity, and low self-esteem. This feeling of dissatisfaction and unhappiness might pervade other elements of your relationship and life.

➢ Remember the ways to connect with yourself to find your truth and balance.

Ways to Deepen Self-Sexual Intimacy.

- ➤ Breathwork.
- ➤ Meditation.
- ➤ Honour yourself.
- ➤ Discover your sexual energy, desires, and pleasures.
- ➤ Improve body image by connecting with your own body.
- ➤ Stretching exercises.
- ➤ Practice booth non-sexual and sexual, self and mutual touch.
- ➤ Explore new ways to express your passion and sexual desire.
- ➤ Energise and deepen your sexual intimacy.
- ➤ Celebrate your own body and personality.

Self-exploration and self-discovery can take time, be gentle and compassionate with yourself as you navigate this journey.

Talk to your partner and express your feelings; you need not feel guilty about seeking intimacy in a relationship. Being intimate gives you the feeling of being close and emotionally connected and supported. Often lack of intimacy can cause partners to feel emotionally abandoned and gradually lose desire and interest in each other, ultimately leading to distancing. So, intimacy is very important for healthy relationships, as it encourages your bond to grow even stronger.

Celebrate the unique qualities and experiences that each layer of intimacy brings and cherish the moments of connection and vulnerability that arise as you explore these different levels of emotional closeness. With a commitment to growth and a willingness to explore, you'll create a relationship that is not only intimate but fulfilling and meaningful as well.

Ultimately, maintaining sexual intimacy and passion in a long-term relationship requires a willingness to be vulnerable, to communicate openly and honestly, and to stay curious and creative. By exploring these strategies and desires, you can deepen your sexual connection with your partner and keep the passion alive over time.

Fear of Intimacy

Fear of intimacy refers to a deep-seated fear of emotional closeness and vulnerability in relationships. This fear can stem from a variety of factors, such as past traumas, relationship disappointments, and negative beliefs about oneself or others.

From a relationship counselling point of view, fear of intimacy can have a significant negative impact on one's ability to form and maintain close relationships. It can manifest in various ways, such as avoiding emotional intimacy altogether, sabotaging relationships when they become too close, or engaging in unhealthy relationship dynamics such as co-dependency or emotional distancing.

In some cases, fear of intimacy can lead to a pattern of relationship avoidance, where individuals may avoid relationships altogether to avoid the discomfort and vulnerability that come with emotional closeness. This can lead to a sense of loneliness and social isolation and can exacerbate feelings of low self-esteem and self-worth.

In addition, fear of intimacy can also impact existing relationships, causing feelings of frustration, resentment, and hurt in partners who feel shut out or rejected by their loved one's inability to connect emotionally.

Fear of intimacy is a psychological condition that can manifest as a persistent avoidance of close relationships, both physical and emotional. It is often rooted in negative experiences from the past, such as abandonment, rejection, or trauma, and can lead to a range of negative consequences, such as loneliness, anxiety, and depression.

Individuals who struggle with fear of intimacy may find it difficult to open up emotionally or to be vulnerable with others. They may avoid close relationships or sabotage them when they feel they are getting too close. They may also struggle with physical intimacy, such as hugging, kissing, or sex, and may feel uncomfortable with physical touch or closeness.

Fear of intimacy can have a significant impact on an individual's quality of life, making it difficult to form meaningful connections with others and leading to feelings of isolation, shame, and low self-esteem. It can also contribute to a range of mental health issues, such as anxiety and depression, and can make it difficult to maintain healthy boundaries or to advocate for one's own needs in relationships.

Ways to overcome the fear of intimacy.

Identify the root of your fear by exploring past experiences or beliefs that may be contributing to it. Take time to reflect on your past experiences and examine how they may have shaped your current beliefs about intimacy. Discuss these with a therapist or close friend who can offer an objective perspective.

Challenge negative beliefs and replace them with positive ones: Create a list of negative beliefs about intimacy and challenge them with evidence-based thoughts that support the idea of healthy relationships. Practice affirmations and repeat them daily to reinforce these positive beliefs.

Understand how your attachment style may impact your relationships.

Make a list of self-care activities that you enjoy and prioritise them in your daily routine. This can include anything from exercise to reading a book to taking a relaxing bath.

Build self-esteem to feel more confident and secure in yourself: Write down positive affirmations about yourself and read them aloud every day. Take small steps towards achieving your goals and celebrate your accomplishments.

Learn to tolerate discomfort and uncertainty in intimate situations; instead of avoiding these uncomfortable feelings, we can learn to sit with them and recognise that they are not permanent. They do not define us, and we have the power to choose how we respond to them. Start by setting aside some time to practice sitting with uncomfortable feelings.

Take responsibility for your emotions and reactions in relationships by focusing on building emotional self-regulation skills so that you can manage your own feelings and responses during intimate experiences. Take a deep breath and pause before reacting to a situation.

Seek help from a mental health professional to address any underlying mental health concerns that may be contributing to your fear of intimacy.

Use visualization exercises to create a safe and nurturing internal space and imagine positive and intimate experiences. Close your eyes and visualize a safe and comfortable space, like a peaceful beach or a cosy cabin in the woods. Practice breathing exercises while visualizing this space to create a sense of calm, safety and intimate experiences with a partner or loved one.

Challenge cognitive distortions, identify any errors or biases in our thinking that can make situations seem worse than they really are and challenge them with more realistic and evidence-based thoughts. For example, black-and-white thinking (seeing things as all good or all bad), jumping to conclusions, overgeneralization, and personalization.

Engage in self-reflection to identify patterns and areas for growth: Spend time reflecting on your past experiences and relationships, identifying patterns and areas for growth. This can help you recognize and address any negative or limiting beliefs about intimacy.

Celebrate small steps towards overcoming your fear of intimacy: Recognize and celebrate the small steps you take towards overcoming your fear of intimacy. Every step, no matter how small, is progress towards a more fulfilling and connected life.

What does intimacy mean to me, and how can I define it in a way that resonates with my personal values and desires?

How satisfied am I with the level of intimacy in my current relationship, and what can I do to enhance it?

What fears or insecurities do I have around intimacy, and how can I work to overcome them and cultivate more trust and openness in my relationships?

How do I practice self-intimacy, and what benefits does it bring me in terms of self-awareness, self-compassion, and self-growth?

In what ways can I deepen my self-intimacy and self-connection, and how can I create more space for my innermost thoughts and emotions to emerge?

What helps me feel more connected to myself and my desires, or to my partner and their desires, and how can I incorporate these practices into my daily life?

What are some of my sexual turn-ons and turn-offs, as well as things I dislike about sex, and how can I communicate them with my partner in a non-judgmental and respectful way?

What are some specific ways I can show love and affection towards myself and my partner that align with our values and deepen our sense of intimacy, and how can I ensure that these actions become a consistent part of our daily routine?

How do I cope with differences in intimacy needs and desires with myself or my partner, and how can I find a middle ground that honours both of our perspectives?

What are some positive and negative impacts that intimacy has on my life or relationship, and how can I manage them in a way that supports my growth and well-being?

What are some activities or experiences I would like to explore with my partner to deepen our intimacy, while prioritizing mutual consent and respect, and how can I communicate my desires and preferences in a way that encourages open and ongoing dialogue, as well as mutual exploration and experimentation?

How do I maintain a healthy balance between giving and receiving intimacy in my relationship, and how can I express gratitude and appreciation for the intimacy that I receive while also honouring my own needs and boundaries?

How do I navigate and deepen the intimacy during challenging times (crisis intimacy)? How can I better support my partner and build a stronger connection during difficult moments?

Do my partner and I actively cultivate both financial and career intimacy in our relationship? Are we working collaboratively to create stability, prosperity, and support each other's professional goals and aspirations?

I am filled with hope and inspiration, knowing that magic and transformation can happen when I open myself up to new experiences and embrace intimacy. Even though it may take time for the effects to become visible, and despite any challenges or discomfort I may face, things will eventually get better. I am confident that every step leads me towards a better and brighter future. I am becoming stronger, wiser, and more resilient, ready to face whatever comes my way. I can achieve great things through trust and perseverance, and I am excited to see where this journey will take me!

CHAPTER 5

Healing Within and Strengthening Relationships

Relationships are an essential part of human life. From the moment we are born, we form connections with others, and these connections continue to shape our lives as we grow and develop. Relationships come in various forms, including romantic, casual, professional, friendships, community, online, and family, and each plays a crucial role in our mental, emotional, and physical well-being.

One of the essential aspects of relationships is the sense of connection and belonging that they provide. Nurturing these connections is essential for our mental, emotional, and physical well-being. Although relationships can be challenging, the effort we put into maintaining them is worth it. Strong relationships can bring us joy, support, and a sense of connection that enriches our lives in countless ways.

Relationships can change and evolve over time. As we grow and develop as individuals, our needs and expectations in relationships may also change. It is essential to communicate openly with our loved ones about these changes, to ensure that our relationships continue to meet our needs and evolve in healthy ways.

Healing relationships with ourselves and others is crucial for our overall well-being. When we experience conflict or hurt in our relationships, it can affect our self-esteem, confidence, and sense of worth. It can also lead to negative self-talk and limiting beliefs that can hold us back from reaching our full potential.

Addressing Hurt Underlying Issues

Hurt is an inevitable part of the human experience. Whether it's physical pain, emotional distress, or mistakes we've made, we all have felt the sting of hurt at some point in our lives.

Experiencing hurt is a natural response to difficult situations, it can manifest in different ways - physical pain, emotional turmoil, or negative actions we may take as a result of our hurt.

Sometimes it can be a challenging experience, and it's important to resist the temptation to turn to unhealthy coping mechanisms like substance abuse or self-harm. Instead, we can learn healthy coping skills that promote self-care and well-being. By taking care of ourselves, we become more resilient and better equipped to handle future challenges.

However, no matter how hurt shows up, we must take responsibility for addressing it head-on This involves recognizing and addressing the underlying issues that may be causing our hurt, such as betrayal that can be deeply hurtful, whether it's someone violating our trust or breaking a promise, unrealistic expectations of ourselves or others, improving communication, understand our and other's needs, setting healthy boundaries, challenging negative self-talk, acknowledging and healing from past hurts, seeking understanding and compromise in differences, manage power imbalances, unresolved conflicts, emotional triggers, lack of trust, and neglect.

Past hurts can linger and influence our current relationships. It's important to acknowledge and heal from these wounds, allowing us to move forward with a sense of clarity and self-awareness.

Differences in values or goals can cause conflicts and hurt feelings. It's important to approach these differences with an open mind and to seek understanding and compromise, finding common ground that honors both ourselves and others.

It's also important to recognize power imbalances, unresolved conflicts, emotional triggers, lack of trust, and neglect as factors that can cause hurt in our relationships.

Most of us often judge ourselves harshly when we experience hurt, forgetting to accept that we all make mistakes and have the potential to cause harm, intentionally or unintentionally. We can approach others with empathy and respect, even when we disagree with their behaviour or actions. Valuing their humanity creates a safe space for healing and growth in ourselves and others.

Cultivating compassion and understanding is not an easy task, and it requires us to let go of our biases and judgments. It is particularly challenging to extend empathy to those who have hurt us or whom we disagree with. However, with practice, we can train ourselves to approach situations with an open mind and heart, leading to a more compassionate and understanding perspective.

Forgiving ourselves is also crucial because it allows us to let go of the harsh self-judgment and criticism that can lead to feelings of shame and guilt. By practicing self-compassion and understanding, we acknowledge our mistakes and failures as part of our journey but not as our identity. This mindset allows us to cultivate a healthier and more positive relationship with ourselves, leading to a more self-empowering and inspirational life.

Similarly, forgiving others requires acknowledging their humanity and potential to make mistakes, leading to a more profound sense of empathy and understanding. It does not mean we condone their behaviour or excuse their actions, but rather we choose to let go of the anger and resentment that can keep us stuck in a cycle of negativity. By extending compassion and understanding towards others, we can cultivate stronger and more authentic relationships based on mutual respect and empathy.

The healing process also requires awareness of our triggers and how they affect our emotions and reactions. Not everyone has difficulties—some have healed from or are working on them.

I know from experience that sometimes we believe it is easier to stay in denial, sweep it under the rug, pretend it did not happen, and maybe even refuse to deal with it. It hurts, it sucks, and it is unfair!

I have been there; I also understand the importance of feeling like we are in control of overwhelming emotions like sadness, loneliness, confusion, fear, and shyness, as they can lead to a lack of self-confidence or act as obstacles in intimate relationships with ourselves and our loved ones.

As part of my Medical Intuitive Certification and training, one of my assignments was to work on my trauma tree. Of course, initially, there was some resistance from my side. I have been deeply working on myself to be on this path helping others since 2008, and I was consciously and unconsciously fully aware of my recent traumas. It took me three days to finish writing it all and honestly reflecting and revisiting every single memory of challenge, hurt, and trauma. I am proud that I did. I have realized that as a baby in my Mum's womb, I was fully aware of my birth Mum's fear and insecurities to bring me into the world. She was a victim of sexual abuse and was not sure who my father was, she also had issues with alcohol and struggled with mental and financial health. I had access to these memories in 2013 during a healing session. However, I had never analyzed how the information that I had access to, had affected my life. I was only six months old when my birth Mum gave me to my godmother who formally adopted me as my Mum.

My first trauma, which was unconscious to me at that time, was linked to most of my struggles and lessons that I had to overcome in life. Doing the exercise, I realized that I had blueprints of confusion on how to show up in the world, a lack of sense of belonging. I felt that I always had to protect myself because somehow at any stage of a relationship with other people, they would break my trust, abuse my vulnerability and generosity, let me down, or stay in my life until it was convenient for them and they got what they thought they needed from the relationship.

I also reflected on the fact that many times as a teenager and adult, when I was being myself and expressing my authenticity, people would say that the way I spoke was too forward (very normal in my culture) and not everyone was pleased with it. Sometimes, I had kept myself to myself to avoid conflict or confrontation and had hidden myself to avoid getting hurt because even if I stood up, something else would happen, and someone else would feel upset just because I was simply being me, I mean myself, and not mean. Well, these were my birth Mum's blueprints, and once I had understood and processed those memories and feelings, a huge healing took place in my inner world.

The healed and empowered version of me is happy to show up to the world with clarity of who I am, I am loved, I embrace my uniqueness, I deserve to be heard, seen, I belong to wherever I choose to be, I am brave and courageous, and I trust that the universe has my back. This version of me doesn't seek validation or approval from others because I know my worth and I am confident in my abilities. I recognize that my journey is unique, and I am grateful for all the experiences that have shaped me into who I am today, and I am excited to see what the future holds. I am committed to living my life to the fullest, being true to myself, inspiring others, and sharing my light with the world.

I know my birth Mum is in spirit because when I moved to the UK, my late husband introduced me to Dave, a medium who was one of his friends. Dave also predicted our wedding even before Angelo had met me in person. It was a very weird experience when I heard from my birth Mum. At that time, I was so scared of anything related to spirits and ghosts. I was so naive that I thought a medium is someone that could see all of our dark and light side.

However, my journey has taken me far. I have not only developed my spirituality, but I also teach people how to develop and connect with their loved ones. In any case, let me share how healing it was for me to have access to a little bit more about my roots and my birth Mum to heal my own relationship.

When Dave asked to speak to me after a delicious teatime and gaining my trust, he started to ask if I knew where my Mum was. I smiled and said that Mum lived in Brazil and that she was well. Then he said no, he was talking about my birth Mum. I was speechless. Then I said I was adopted and had no contact or any information about her.

Dave shared that she was in spirit and that she wanted me to forgive her. She explained that she did the best for me because she knew she could not be the Mum that I deserved or give me the foundations to become who I am today. She mentioned that seeing the wonderful woman I had become reassured her that she had made the right decision. She was struggling to take care of herself, let alone a child. She also mentioned that she had passed away in a car accident and provided plenty of evidence to show that she was very much aware of how my life has been. As part of the evidence, Dave could even describe how my wedding dress would be, both of them, and that Mum would be there as she always had been since transitioning to the spirit world.

I forgave my Mum straight away; I couldn't feel anger all these years because I understood she was a victim and had her own struggles. She did the best she could with the knowledge she had. The Mum she chose to raise me gave me not just a big and loving family but also strong foundations.

It was because of my inner work and healing story that I could grow up with a new family, feel unconditional love, learn valuable lessons from Mum and Dad that both in their own as role models have inspired through their life lessons of overcoming challenges, building resilience, strength, innovation, and care for others.

Many years later, after developing my mediumship abilities, I was able to reconnect with my birth Mum, and more healing took place. I understand that these spiritual experiences may sound strange; they certainly did to me and were even a bit scary before I made the decision to connect with my grandfather, who was like a father to me. Developing my mediumship abilities was a decision that forever changed my life and has allowed me to positively impact others by sharing my experiences and knowledge.

On an informative note, developing psychic abilities and mediumship is not exclusive to gifted individuals. With time, developing spiritual qualities, effort, patience, practice, love, commitment and personal responsibility, anyone can learn to develop these abilities.

Opening up to my spirituality took my relationship with myself to a deeper level of growth, maturity, fulfilment, love, healing and inner peace that I never thought would be possible. We all have stories and struggles in life, we all are special somehow, and it is never too late to find meaningful ways to feel alive and live life on your terms and have the healthy relationship we deserve.

Never lose Hope and Faith in yourself, no matter what you may be going through. I get it; sometimes only words depending on the situation, may not be enough but please shout out for help and trust that the universe will somehow answer your call as they have done for me and millions of people who, like me, and you, and those dear to you and even people that had to overcome challenges or even lose everything (like I did, not only once but twice) and have had to find its way to heal, grow, rediscover themselves, innovate and reawaken to life.

If I could find ways to feel alive to rediscover and reconnect with myself, my inner strength, and resilience, find peace, and heal, so can you. You can overcome anything that may be holding you back—inspire yourself and, with time, others around you.

So, if you're feeling hurt right now, know that you have the power to take ownership of your healing journey, cultivate self-awareness, empathy, and effective communication skills, learn healthy coping mechanisms that promote self-care and well-being and choose to respond with strength, courage, and compassion. You can let hurt/pain define you and hold you back, or you can use it as a catalyst for growth and emerge from your struggles even stronger, resilient, and wiser than you ever thought possible. The choice is yours.

Only you know what you have experienced that caused an imbalance in your intimate relationship with yourself and others. Sometimes people have to deal with a sexual problem (illness, disabilities, medications, physical numbness, lack of arousal, difficulties in achieving orgasm, vaginismus and painful sex, erection issues, freezing/disassociation, and so on) or lack of the ability to meet needs for certainty, variety, significance, connection/love, growth, and contribution or may have any other emotional blockage.

Some individuals may find themselves trapped in a cycle of repeating patterns and attracting similar relationships in their lives, either because they have not done their inner work and taken responsibility for their actions, or because they may not have a clear understanding of what a healthy and sexual relationship involves or does involve, especially if they have experienced trauma or have not had access to comprehensive sex education.

A healthy and sexual relationship does NOT involve:

- Disrespect.
- Criticism and Ridicule.
- Narcissistic or Controlling Behavior.
- Poor Communication.
- Lack of trust.
- Emotional abuse.
- Dishonesty.
- Lack of boundaries.
- Verbal Abuse.
- Disagreement on Major Values.
- Trying to Change You.
- Co-dependency Behavior.
- Lack of emotional support.
- Substance Abuse.
- Loss of Respect.
- Jealousy and Insecurity.
- Passive Aggressive Behavior.
- Inability to Forgive.
- Isolation.
- Unrealistic expectations.
- Angry behavior.
- Sexually Focused.
- Competition.
- Hatred or hostility.

- Betrayal.
- Feeling trapped.
- Hostility.
- Possessiveness.
- Deflecting responsibility.
- Confrontational Attitude.
- Diminishes your self-worth.
- Avoidance.
- Betrayal.
- Manipulation.
- Blame.
- Cultural abuse.
- Alcohol or drug abuse.
- Abuse of Kindness.
- Becoming overprotective.
- Arguments that escalate to ultimatums or threats.
- Dismiss each other emotions.
- Feeling lonely when you're together.
- Lack of compromise and quality time together.
- Disrespect and blame towards Ex-partners.
- Lack of engagement when you speak about your interests and projects.
- Reintroduce past disagreements in current conflicts.
- Consistent jealousy and insecurity.
- Lack of physical affection (rarely kiss, touch, hug or smile at each other).
- Any kind of sexually abusive situation.
- Disrespecting "NO" consent and boundaries.
- Being disgusted with your partner, rejecting them.
- Absence of emotional intimacy.
- Having to fake sexual enjoyment.
- Being unable to comfort your partner.
- Having sex when not fully alert.
- Having sex outside a primary relationship or promiscuous sex without your partner's consent to be in an open relationship.

➢ Acting in sexually demanding or exploitative ways.

➢ Using abusive sexual fantasies or pornography.

➢ Combining sex and emotional or physical abuse.

➢ Or engaging in compulsive masturbation.

And guess what? It is not about how many times you have sex or even how often you orgasm.

This is not an exhaustive list. Perhaps you are still trying to find some answers to understand where you are in your sexual healing journey and your level of commitment to having a healthy and sexual relationship and trying to understand what lessons you have learned from your past experiences. Maybe you can still feel certain emotions, see those physical or emotional scars, and envision the scene so vividly in your mind.

It is okay to feel frustration, sadness, anger, or cry about it. You have every right to. You may have been through an unpleasant or unexpected experience. Everyone reacts differently to situations they perceive as threatening their life, bodily integrity, or sanity.

Only you know when you feel ready to talk about it. When you feel you have the strength to sit with those emotions, there is no shame in asking and accepting help. Consider reaching out for support and starting your healing journey. Do not choose to stay in denial, and do not try to suppress and repress these feelings.

Some people grow up never feeling as though they can talk about their feelings or express themselves, so they continue the pattern of silence and denial—it is what is familiar to them. But the past does not define the present, who we are, or our future. Only you can permit yourself to start the healing process, allowing you to start the journey to reclaim your power.

Trust me, resilience could have been my middle name. I know the healing journey can be quite painful and requires time, courage, kindness, self-love, acceptance, forgiveness, and willingness to understand lessons, heal the wounds and give a more empowering meaning to what has happened. Let go of what or who does not serve any purpose in our lives anymore. Ideally, forgive whatever may have happened and send them love and move on, not for them, but for you.

For over a decade, I have done a lot of inner work and studied and practiced many different healing modalities, from five Teacher Masters in Reiki to Pure energy healing, Shamanic, Dialectical Behavior Therapy, Past life regressions, Hypnotherapy, Cognitive Behavioral Therapy, Acceptance and Commitment Therapy, Spiritual and Trance healing and others. I have learned through my healing journey that the process can have many different layers and root causes and sometimes we may think we have dealt with a situation, but there might still be some subconscious and energetic work that needs to be done. However, finding peace within and reconnecting with our true selves is extremely rewarding.

Once awake and aware, we can empower ourselves to engage in new, healthy coping mechanisms instead of the old, ineffective ones that don't work to bring harmony or oneness to the relationship. New coping mechanisms require transparency and vulnerability.

Simple Steps to Acknowledge Your Blockages

1. Sit quietly with your thoughts and emotions.
2. Avoid projecting the past on the present.
3. Be kind to yourself, especially if you are blaming yourself for not being able to let go of unpleasant memories or circumstances. Give yourself love, self-compassion, and kindness.
4. Let your thoughts and emotions flow through you, and do not interrupt them.
5. How do you feel when you think about that upsetting or traumatic event? How would you like to feel instead? Write down the thoughts and emotions that come to you as you mentally relive the experience.
6. Cross the things off your list you would like to let go of.
7. Bring yourself back to the present whenever you think about someone or a situation that has brought you sorrow. Then concentrate on your present moment.
8. Now, you should have clarity on what emotions and thoughts you need to work through.

9. Create a positive mantra to help you overcome your negative thoughts.
10. Write a list of ways you want to practice self-care when you are in pain. While it can feel like there is nothing else to do but hurt, start by taking baby steps if you feel you need them.
11. Set boundaries, say no, do the things that do not bring you safety, pleasure, and comfort, and respond to your needs first.

After acknowledging that you need healing, it is time to accept it and its consequences. This is usually when we may feel overwhelmed and doubtful. Most of the time, it is because we feel lost and confused, like we have lost our identity—this is why it is so important to ask for help from a qualified professional.

I have compiled some steps that can assist you in your path when you need to deal with overpowering emotions.

➢ Recognize that you have had an upsetting or terrifying encounter, and you will react emotionally to it.
➢ Recognize that you will not feel like your typical self for a period of time, but this will pass.
➢ Remind yourself that you are managing daily—try not to get upset or frustrated with yourself if you cannot complete tasks as well or efficiently as you would like.
➢ Do not use alcohol or drugs as a coping mechanism to deal with your issues.
➢ Wait until you feel better before making important decisions or changes in your life.
➢ Do not try to block out what has happened; face it gradually.
➢ Do not keep your emotions bottled up; talk to someone who can help and understand you.
➢ Try to stick to your routine and stay busy.
➢ Do not make a point of avoiding specific places or activities.
➢ Take your time if you need it until you feel you can create a new routine that will allow you to return to your life commitments.
➢ If you are tired, make sure you schedule a time to rest.

➢ Schedule regular exercise to help relieve tension in your body and mind.

➢ Assist your family and friends by letting them know what you need, whether it is a break or someone to chat with.

➢ Unwind—try relaxation techniques like yoga, breathing, or meditation, or do things you enjoy.

➢ Express your emotions as they emerge. Talk about them with someone or write them down.

➢ Try to confront memories or sensations that are triggered by the trauma. Consider them, then set them aside. If it triggers other memories, try to isolate them from the current issue and deal with them independently.

It is possible to make a deliberate decision to stay in the past, just as it is possible to make a conscious decision to let go.

You can overcome an unpleasant blockage/situation by letting go of your pains from a past that has been haunting you in your present. These pains are the obstacles holding you back from enjoying intimacy with yourself and your loved ones.

When there is trauma involved, it demands careful attention and treatment, as it can have a devastating impact on relationships and have long-term consequences. Treatment, on the other hand, can assist in reducing the risks and educate individuals and or couples on how to care for each other more deeply. It can help reduce the danger of isolation and restore hope in a relationship. It also creates a safe environment for talking about those events and the sentiments that come with them.

Understanding how to look after yourself and those dearest to you, particularly intimate partners, can make the difference between healing and stagnation.

In my case, even with all the tools and wisdom I have, when I had to deal with my traumatic experience, if I had not asked for help, I would not be here today, feeling fully back in my power and aligned with my purpose. I had to have someone that I trusted in some of my healing sessions, to ask me questions or oversee the work that I was able to do through trance healing, regression, and hypnosis, as in my case, the healing was required to be on an energetic, soul, subconscious, and spiritual level.

Whatever situation you find yourself in, whenever you are unsure . . . Apply love. Show love. Be love.

Eventually, we feel awakened. We fall in love with ourselves and feel the power of LOVE. The one that heals even the deepest of wounds. We realise that we are no longer the same person who was afraid of weakened emotions. We create healthy boundaries and surround ourselves with what resonates with us—a beautiful sign of maturity. When it happens, we understand that we are the only ones responsible for healing our inner world and decide to create an empowering reality, choosing to be our authentic selves. We learn to let go of whatever does not serve our highest good. When we achieve this stage, we know we are braver and more resilient than ever.

"I have pride in everything I have overcome to get me to this moment."

We all appreciate and deserve to be with someone we know loves us unconditionally, and no matter what, they will be there for us. Being truthful to our values, having behaviors matching our words, consistent responses, and commitment are also essential to make a relationship work, while a sense of uncertainty, risk-taking and variety are important to sustaining passion.

Life, as we all know, can also get in the way and affect our moods, energy levels and capacity to have quality time for ourselves or our relationships. When it happens, the desire to make love, have sex, or even have a quickie can be put aside. During this time, it is important to have patience, apply self-love, kindness and care, rest, and renew your energy levels. If you are in a relationship, give the right dose of affection, support and empathy. Hugs, a smile, being present, cooking your lover's favorite food and sometimes doing nothing together can have a powerful outcome. If required, give the space your partner may need.

A healthy and sexual relationship DOES involve:

- ✓ Owning your feelings.
- ✓ Accountability for your happiness.

✓ Understand each other's needs, preferences, and communication styles.

✓ Open communication and effective listening, where you both can be honest about your expectations, give each other reassurance, work through problems together, trust each other, and feel emotionally safe and respected.

✓ Consult one another before making decisions, and approach everything as a team with the intent of supporting each other.

✓ Understand that you and your partner are two separate entities, so do not lose yourself or allow your lover to lose himself/herself/ themselves.

✓ Connection, presence, creativity, and passion are ongoing and renewed.

✓ There is acceptance and respect for each other's boundaries.

✓ Forgiveness, when necessary.

✓ It brings both of you joy, playfulness and adventure.

✓ You can do things you like to do together or apart, honoring individuality.

✓ Make each other feel seen, desired, sexy, and comfortable to say what each other want.

✓ Guilt and worry for turning down sex or for how often it happens do not exist.

✓ Mutual feelings and desired outcomes are satisfied.

✓ Release expectations and allow surprise and spontaneity.

✓ Both partners can orgasm, improve, and discover erogenous zones.

✓ Affection and connection are beyond the bedroom.

✓ Allowing space for friendship, romance, sensuality, sacredness, energy, growth, maturity, inspiration, contribution, innovation, naughtiness…

✓ Feels balanced, and you both feel a close, intimate, and spiritual bond.

Independent of whether you're single or in a relationship, the affirmations below are from me to you. Do us a favor and read them out loud to yourself, and if you like, use them as your daily affirmation. These are words that we would love to hear from our partners, but most of the time, we do not say them to ourselves, even as we look ourselves in the mirror.

I love you.

I believe you.

I appreciate you.

You inspire me.

Thank you for listening and seeing me. It means a lot.

I love how you show up for me when I really need you.

You are my best friend. You encourage me when I'm

doubtful and inspire me to be my best self.

I feel very lucky to have you in my life.

You are amazing.

I am really proud of you.

My life is so much better with you in it.

Thank you.

I love you and I always will.

How have my past experiences impacted the way I view myself, and what steps can I take to heal those wounds and shift to more positive beliefs and thought patterns?

Are there any negative coping mechanisms or behaviors do I engage in to avoid difficult emotions, and how can I replace them with healthier alternatives that promote healing and growth?

How can I let go of any unhealthy relationships or dynamics in my life that may be holding me back from reaching my full potential, and how can I cultivate healthier relationships moving forward?

In what ways can I be more present and engaged with my loved ones during difficult moments, and what can I do to strengthen those relationships?

What do I need to let go of in order to move forward and improve my relationships, and how can I take ownership of my role in maintaining and fostering healthy relationships?

How can I continue to develop my self-awareness and emotional intelligence to navigate my relationships with more confidence and ease, and what resources or practices can I utilize to support my growth in these areas?

How can I empower myself to navigate conflicts or differences in opinion with people dear to me in a way that promotes healing and growth rather than further division, and what communication skills can I develop to support this process?

How can I cultivate greater empathy towards myself and others to build stronger, healthier relationships, and what steps can I take to practice active listening and validate the emotions and perspectives of those around me?

How can I prioritize my own self-care and personal growth while also nurturing my relationships, and what steps can I take to build a stronger foundation of trust and overcome any trust issues or insecurities that may be impacting my relationships?

In what ways can I take ownership of my role in improving the overall health and wellbeing of my relationships, and what actionable steps can I commit to taking to achieve this?

Have I experienced situations where expressing my authenticity and speaking my mind led to conflict or confrontation? How did I react to these situations, and did I hide or suppress myself to avoid getting hurt.

Am I taking responsibility for addressing and healing from the underlying issues causing my hurt? Have I identified and acknowledged factors such as betrayal, unrealistic expectations, communication issues, trust issues, unresolved conflicts, or emotional triggers?

I cherish my heart and love myself deeply. I am committed to improving how I feel about myself daily. I am growing in self-love and acceptance every day, and my body and mind reflect this positive energy. In the mirror, I see the love I create within myself. I am proud of who I am and determined to grow even more. Every moment brings me closer to my true essence, and I am excited to discover my full potential. My self-love and positivity give me the strength to achieve anything I set my mind to. I am taking care of myself from the inside out, and my self-worth, self-compassion, and self-esteem are increasing daily.

CHAPTER 6

Your Own Sexuality

Sexuality is about how we experience and express our feelings, thoughts, attractions, behaviours, sensuality, intimacy, spirituality, reproduction, identity and preferences sexually. It is diverse and personal, and it is an essential part of who we are, embracing ourselves in all aspects—mind, body, and spirit.

Our sexuality is like a mirror reflecting who we are as people. It's a mix of what we desire, how we feel, and how we connect with others. It's unique to each of us, like a fingerprint. Sexuality isn't just about the physical side of things. It's a part of our identity, influencing our choices, our relationships, and how we fit into the world around us.

Understanding your own sexuality can be a complex process, and it's okay if you don't fully grasp it. Your sexuality is a part of you, always present, whether you're fully aware of it or not.

Feeling guilt and shame about having a period, our physical weight, shape, your style, clothes, make-up, hair, or size, being diagnosed with a sexually transmitted illness (STI), or our gender identity or sexual orientation are all examples of the sexual stigma that impacts people's mental well-being (some consequences are tendencies to disorders like unhealthy eating, eating disorders, self-harming, unhealthy behavior, developing poor self-esteem and criticism, and so on), social health, and their professional lives.

From a young age, we are exposed to images of idealized or unrealistic bodies. Some do not fall into the trap of comparing themselves to others, while others are happy to embrace themselves and their bodies, while some people feel the pressure to look a certain way or want to match their ideal body type.

It is normal to hear comments about bodies and appearance; however, there is a big difference when someone close to us makes an innocent comment concerned about our health, pointing out that we may have lost or gained weight, and people who act from a place of ignorance with the intention to cause insecurity and body shame.

We live in a very repressed culture when it comes to our sexuality. It is a world that also has the judgment and lack of acceptance of differences learned from our caregivers, media (social media, news/movies/television, educational institutions), colleagues, friends, and society that can make people feel insecure, scared, unhappy, unable to express their feelings, and disempowered.

Life would be so much easier if people could live without projecting their judgment, insecurities, and fears onto the other person. Everyone has a dark side and bad days, and no one deserves to have fingers pointed at them, be exposed, be shamed, be exposed to social media or public humiliation, or have their wounds displayed in public unless the person themselves feels it is appropriate to share it

Social media organizations, some influencers, product/services advertisers, or people looking for significance instead of serving from a place of love and integrity try to insert themselves in a way that they're always the center of people's attention or try to manipulate them to gain their attention, usually by finding or creating a pain point and then offering a solution, making you believe they are doing a disservice if they do not sell you their products or services that will make you feel good about the possibility of gaining the ideal body and appearance dictated by them..

I have not watched the news for over fifteen years, and I do stay as much as possible away from social media because I have become aware of how much emotional damage can cause to sensitive people. I am happy with my body and I choose to prioritize myself, my family, my energy and practice a lot of self-care to be in a position where my cup is full and balanced again so I can be at service helping others. This is my choice. It is what I know benefits my journey. How about you? Are you aware of how much influence the media and others may have over you and your daily routine? You are the one who knows about your needs, why you spend your time following certain people, news, or social channels, and how your routine and the people that you choose to have in your life are helping you with your growth or not. It is your choice to create the environment and routine that will suit your needs and decide whom you choose to be in your life and be there for you as you are for others.

When someone experiences having grown up with a lot of conditioning, where everything that they were feeling was wrong, their preferences, attractions or identity were questionable or inappropriate, those conditioning words or sentences can contribute to the way they express their sexuality in the world, usually with repression, projection, denial, and this is without even the mention of mental health issues that can be developed over the years.

When you live a life where your authentic sexual self has the freedom to express itself, there are so many things you can do, while many people in the world do not live free and feel so trapped because they feel they can't express their sexuality the way they want to express it. They can't love whom they want to love, or they may lack an understanding of their own sexuality. They may feel fear, pain, and repression even in other areas of their life. So, when they see others authentically expressing their sexuality, going against the norm, it makes them consciously, mostly unconsciously, feel that they're not doing that, and most of the time, they are unaware of what is causing their own triggers.

How many people suffer from that? And how many people suffer because they're called names like gay, bi, lesbian, fag, queer and so on. They are victims of identity hate crime. There's a lot of suffering and pain caused by ignorance and statements that are made and things that people may feel that they have to fight against in the world.

People can only understand and love others to the degree they understand and love themselves. Some people feel safe through their own rules and guidelines about what is good, what is bad, what's right and what is wrong. They only appreciate you if you're doing what they want you to do.

Others may express love verbally, but it might be based on their own unique understanding. Life can be more challenging when you don't conform to the identity they expect, and their judgments and advice often stem from fear, yet ultimately it can come from a place of care.

Be aware of negative feelings like rejection, usually when a person rejects themselves, they seek external validation from others to let them know they are okay. So it's important that people have their own self-esteem and their own ability to tell themselves; I am doing my best or just enough for today, I am enjoying all the opportunities I have to explore and overcome new challenges because I know that I am smart, I have beauty within, I embrace my sexuality, I know I am worth it and I choose to release any worries and live in the present moment because all is well in my inner world.

The best we can do is be aware of our internal judgement and shift all we cannot control, shifting our energy, our thoughts; by the way, a thought is so powerful that when we have a thought bigger than ourselves, we can experience ourselves having an out of body experience, see themselves in a different place ... Just a thought can cause orgasmic shivers. I know, right? Have you thought about it? I can see smiles as I write this.

We have no control over what other people say about us or how they perceive us. To be honest, who cares? Are they paying all your bills or living your life? Do they know how it really feels to be in your skin and to be yourself twenty-four hours a day? No one should have any power over you. So why not choose to release any attachments and allow ourselves to make our inner world a better place?

Love, acceptance, self-compassion, and unconditional positive regard start with us, we cannot control the external world, but we can choose how we want our inner world to be and transform it.

You have the power to create such a place of acceptance, unconditional love and peace inside yourself without the need to wait for the world to accept it because you are the one that can make the conscious choice to make your inner world a better one for you and those whom you choose to have in your life, those that you know love and accept you as you are.

Claim any emotional baggage you may have, don't give to somebody else; claim it, accept it, understand the lessons, heal it, let it go, listen to hear and understand yourself and others and speak with self-compassion when you do; you feel a sense of personal power.

No one likes to enter into a relationship with someone with emotional baggage and fears; they never feel safe or can fully open their hearts or be themselves because they have not done the inner work, and the chances that you can build a strong foundation are quite low.

Let's explore more about sexuality and sexual self-awareness and ways that may help you to feel good about yourself.

Sex is exciting. It is because our parents had sex that we were born. Sex is important not only for reproduction but for our overall health. It can help to reduce stress, lower blood pressure, and even increase our memory, reduce pain, can be orgasmic and boost our self-esteem when we permit ourselves to start a self-discovery and exploration to enjoy with respect and consent the attraction, show attention, and affection, be aware of our desires, triggers, feelings, turn on, turn off, our likes, dislikes and needs.

Independently of your identity and as part of your process to explore self-intimacy, self-love, and sexual awareness, get familiar with your whole body in the mirror.

Let's be honest; when do we ever talk about this? It's not a typical subject that we discuss, not even with our best friend (s), but it can be so helpful for anyone's health to understand how our body works and what it looks like and embrace it with love, whatever the size, shape, and colour. It is yours to appreciate and celebrate, don't wait for anyone to do it for you!

Be comfortable with who you are and familiar with your anatomy. If you don't know where to begin, there are plenty of resources available to help you learn more about your sexual anatomy.

Replace any judgement, embarrassment, and shameful thoughts with a big smile, recognising that there is a beauty within you that you can only see when you come from a place of love, gratitude, and acceptance.

Accept that each body is unique in its appearance and purpose and that the standard for a body is best defined by the individual to whom it belongs, not by society. It's all about becoming more at ease with yourself, on both the giving and receiving aspects, allowing you to learn to open yourself up to self-intimacy and claim your sexual power discovering what makes you happy, excited, satisfied, or fulfilled.

I understand that sometimes it is easy to say than feel it. Be kind to yourself and have self-compassion, release any expectations, and enjoy your intimate time with your body. When we ignore or invalidate how we feel, we are telling ourselves that our feelings are not important. It can take time to accept and commit to new health changes if that's what you want to do.

Whenever you feel ready to explore, make sure that you have quality time and that you will not be disturbed.

Pay attention to different parts of your body and get familiar with the look and feel of your skin, breast, and genitals. This practice also helps you recognize when something has changed and answer any questions your doctor may have if you need an examination.

Take a few minutes to focus on your body and your attention on your sexual feelings. You can do this by relaxing, taking deep breaths, or just focusing on your own body. You can stimulate yourself in different ways, such as using a vibrator or a dildo if you already have explored with your touch, your fingers and explore your erogenous zones, the mouth, lips, earlobes, scalp, abdomen, breasts, nipples, inner thighs, lower abdomen/pubic area, the area behind the knees, the perineum or genitals and all the way down to the toes noticing the parts of the body that feel good to touch. Every part can be a source of pleasure. Listen to your body and forget what you may have read or learned from others' experiences. Give yourself permission to feel, explore different areas and intense your focus on the feelings that you have. This will help you to know what types of stimulation you enjoy, what you like and what you don't like, and how to reach orgasm. Experiment with different types of touch, different speeds, and different levels of pressure. Find plenty of ways to ensure the parts you feel more aroused about get played with more often.

Another way to learn a lot about your body is by paying attention to your sexual response during foreplay, where you go beyond touch exploration and can explore kissing, positions, feathers, fruits, objects, or a more spiritual connection through tantra or other ways you may like to explore making love, having sex and orgasms with your partner.

Many people masturbate because it helps them sleep at night better, relax and de-stress or because they feel uncomfortable or pain while having sex with their partners. Stress, puberty, sexual abuse, or mental illness can cause masturbation to become a problem. Please consider talking to your doctor about it. It is important that you get the right treatment for the problem.

You and your lover can also work together to have a healthy relationship that isn't focused on sex and help each other with building confidence and self-esteem, as they have a big impact on the things we do and how able we are to ask for what we want and like.

Do Things That Make You Feel Good, Gorgeous or Sensual

Celebrate moments that bring you happiness, beauty, or a sense of connection with yourself. Think about things that truly make you happy and alive.

Sometimes, treating yourself to something nice, such as new clothes, a fresh haircut, a delightful meal at your favorite restaurant, or cooking something special at home, or embarking on a spontaneous day trip to explore a nearby town or city you haven't visited before, or indulging in a spa day, can make you feel beautiful both inside and out.

When you engage in any activity that you feel joy, it's not just enjoyable; it's also a way of expressing self-love. It's about appreciating yourself and building confidence. Feeling good about yourself doesn't mean fitting into any special rules; it's about liking yourself and nurturing self-assurance.

Life is a continuous journey of discovery and transformation. Something I have learned from my healing journey through grief is that even when we find ourselves at a low point in life, where it feels like the end, we can discover that we have choices. We can choose to explore the potential to rediscover life's vitality and intimacy. This reawakening occurs when we cultivate self-love, take full responsibility for our lives, and reestablish a profound connection with our body, mind, and spirit

With time, we grant ourselves permission to embrace a deeper and more fulfilling relationship with ourselves. This, in turn, allows us to once again open our hearts to the infinite ways that can make us feel joyful, attractive, and sensual—both for our own well-being and for the enrichment of our connections.

Wherever you find yourself on your journey of embracing your unique sexuality, stand authentically in your truth. Release the need to take things personally, to deny, or to repress. Recognize that many others share similar values and experiences, but each person's story is unique. You are living your own narrative, and you can't walk in anyone else's shoes. When you encounter situations or individuals that trigger feelings of insecurity, confidently assert your healthy boundaries.

Your uniqueness transcends societal constructs and expectations. You are a unique blend of desires and attractions. Embrace the spectrum of your sexuality, and know that it's beautiful in its complexity. When you carry yourself with confidence and self-assuredness, it's not just attractive; it's empowering.

Always remember to show love and kindness to yourself, because you are truly deserving of love, happiness, and fulfillment exactly as you are. Your feelings, desires, and who you are as a whole person are important, and you should take joy in celebrating them.

Most importantly, trust in yourself. Believe deeply that you are valuable just the way you are and that you deserve all the good things life has to offer. You're a unique and special person, and your journey through life is a precious gift.

Space for Self-Reflection

How do I define my own sexual identity, and what aspects of it are most important to me? What do I believe are the essential components of a healthy sexual identity?

Have I experienced body shaming or negative comments about my body or sexuality? How can I process these experiences and learn to separate my self-worth from the opinions of others and learn to love and accept myself fully, without judgment or shame?

Are there any parts of myself that I have tried to deny or repress sexually? How can I acknowledge and embrace these aspects of myself in a way that feels safe and empowering?

How can I overcome any shame or guilt I may have about my sexual desires and preferences, and embrace them fully in my relationship?

What aspects of myself do I need to embrace and why? How can I celebrate my unique qualities and appreciate my strengths and weaknesses as part of my journey of self-discovery and growth?

Can I reflect on the personality traits and values that I find attractive in a potential partner? Do these traits align with my own values and desires? How can I take steps towards personal growth and becoming more aligned with what I seek in a partner?

What would a perfect date with me look like? How can I prioritize self-care and self-love as part of my journey of self-discovery and growth?

Based on my current understanding of myself and my sexuality, can I reflect on past experiences where I may have denied or repressed parts of myself that others noticed? How can I use this insight to embrace and celebrate all aspects of myself moving forward?

Write a list of at least twenty things (yes, 20!) that you value and love about yourself, including qualities that make you feel happy, vibrant, energized, and sexy.

Write a list of positive and empowering affirmations that make you feel the same way. Keep this list close to your mirror and repeat these affirmations to yourself every morning and evening with intention, enthusiasm, and belief.

Can I let go of external judgments and expectations and create a safe space for my authentic sexual self to express and thrive? Am I committed to cultivating a positive and empowering relationship with my own sexuality?

Am I aware of how conditioning and societal judgments have influenced my sexuality, and am I ready to question and reshape those beliefs? Can I nurture a deep sense of self-acceptance, self-compassion, and self-love when it comes to my body and sexual identity?

I show myself kindness, affection, love, acceptance, and respect, embracing all parts of my identity, including my sensuality.

Through connecting with my body and desires, I find strength, joy, and meaningful relationships. I confidently communicate my needs and boundaries with respect for myself and others.

I view physical intimacy as a natural and restorative experience, approaching it with care and empathy. When I listen and trust the wisdom of my body's signals, I explore new levels of pleasure and intimacy, always remaining open to discovering new aspects of myself.

CHAPTER 7

Deepening Your Connections

Embodiment is a holistic approach to personal growth and development that integrates the body, mind, and spirit. It recognizes that the body is not just a physical vessel, but also a source of information, wisdom, and insight. It is the felt sense of being alive and present in the moment, it is about developing a deeper connection with oneself and one's physical experiences through a transformative journey that invites us to explore the depths of our being and unlock our fullest potential.

At the core of embodiment is the understanding that our bodies and minds are intimately connected. Our way of being in the world shapes our perceptions, values, and goals, and our physical sensations as emotional experiences are intertwined. By tuning into our bodies and becoming more aware of our sensations, we unlock our creativity. We feel encouraged to explore ways of expressing ourselves, cultivate self-awareness, self-acceptance, and self-compassion, which have a profound impact on our ability to connect with others and cultivate intimacy.

When we become more attuned to our physical sensations, emotions, and thoughts, we can cultivate a deeper understanding of ourselves and our needs., unlock the potential for pleasure, love, and healthy bonds, and experience a sense of connection to something greater than us. We can cultivate empathetic communication, healthy boundaries, meaningful connections, and experience the joy and fulfillment of deep, intimate, and loving relationships and transform our lives in countless ways, becoming more fully present, engaged, and alive.

By paying attention to bodily sensations, we can begin to recognize patterns of tension or discomfort, learning how to release them. Through the utilization of embodiment techniques, we can cultivate a stronger connection between our mind and body, exploring how our physical experiences can affect our emotions and thoughts, leading to a greater understanding of how these experiences may manifest in our relationships. It can also provide insight into our unconscious habits, helping us break free from unhelpful patterns and address the impact of stress and trauma, ultimately leading to a more balanced, fulfilling, and joyful life.

The techniques promote relaxation and a sense of calmness, helping to reduce stress, and anxiety and address the impact of stress and trauma. It can also improve our flexibility, strength, and balance, as well as boost our immune system and enhance other bodily functions.

There are many benefits that can be enjoyed by both individuals and couples.

While practices like Tai chi, Aikido, and Yoga are fantastic examples of embodiment techniques that can be done **solo**, there are numerous other suggestions below to consider.

- Body mapping: Is a practice that can help you connect with your body on a deeper level, including the sensations of your skin, muscles, and bones. Through touch, massage, and exploration, you can become more aware of the areas that feel good, uncomfortable, or even painful. By tuning into the physical sensations of your body, you can gain a better understanding of your own desires and preferences and empower yourself to take charge of your own sexual satisfaction and enhance your overall well-being.
- Creative Expression: Engage in some form of creative expression, whether it's painting, writing, singing, or dancing. Allow yourself to express your emotions and thoughts in a way that feels authentic and

meaningful to you. This practice can help you to connect with your inner self and to express your unique voice and perspective.

- The Grounding technique focuses on your breath and the sensation of your feet on the ground. This can help you to Anchor yourself in the present moment and become more aware of your body and can be helpful in times of stress or anxiety.

- Mindful Touch: Spend some time each day touching your body in a gentle and loving way. You can do this through self-massage, applying lotion to your skin, or simply placing your hands on different parts of your body. This practice can help you to cultivate a sense of self-care and nurturing, and to deepen your connection to your physical self.

- Breathing Practice: Spend some time each day practicing deep, slow breathing. As you breathe, focus on accepting whatever thoughts, feelings, or sensations arise in your body, without judgment or the need to change anything. This practice can help you to cultivate a sense of calm and centeredness, and to accept whatever arises in your body and mind.

- Nature Connection: Spend time in nature and focus on connecting with your body and the natural world around you. This could be as simple as taking a walk in a park, hiking or spending time gardening, the intention is to paying attention to the sights, sounds, movements and sensations around you.

- Mindful Reading: Read a book mindfully, paying close attention to the words and the story. This practice can help you to cultivate a sense of presence and awareness, and to connect with the emotions and experiences of the characters in the story.

- Body Movement: Move your body in ways that feel good to you. This can be through yoga, stretching, dancing, or any other form of movement that feels enjoyable and nourishing to your body. This practice can help you to connect with your body, and to cultivate a sense of joy and pleasure in your physical self.

- Sensual Pleasure: Explore your senses through pleasurable experiences. This can be through indulging in your favorite foods, wearing clothes that feel good on your body, or engaging in activities that bring you pleasure, such as taking a warm bath or getting a massage. This practice can help you to cultivate a sense of sensuality and pleasure in your body.

- Mindful Eating: Take the time to really savor and appreciate your food. Focus on the taste, texture, and aroma of each bite.
- Body Gratitude: Take some time each day to express gratitude for your body. You can do this through journaling, affirmations, or simply saying thank you to your body. This practice can help you to cultivate a sense of appreciation for your body, and to shift your focus from self-criticism to self-love.

Many couples find that their relationship improves when they start doing exercises that focus on embodiment, it can be a lot of fun and deepen their connection. Here are examples of different exercises that you can try with your partner. Be sure to have plenty of laughs, make memories, and enjoy the experience!

- Eye Gazing: Sit facing your partner and gaze into each other's eyes without speaking. Notice any emotions that arise and allow yourself to fully experience them.
- Sensory Deprivation: Blindfold one partner and guide them through a sensory experience. This could include touching different textures, tasting different foods, or smelling different scents.
- Partnered Breathing: Sit facing your partner and synchronize your breath. Inhale and exhale together, focusing on the sensations of your breath in your body.
- Laughter Yoga: Laughing together is a great way to bond and reduce stress. You can follow along with a laughter yoga video or just start laughing together and see where it takes you.
- Sensual Dance: Put on some music and dance together in a sensual way. Focus on moving your bodies in a way that feels good to you and your partner.

- Self-Exploration: Take turns exploring your own bodies in front of your partner. Use touch and movement to explore your body and express your sensuality.
- Guided Visualization: Take turns leading each other through a guided visualization. This could be anything from imagining a relaxing beach scene to visualizing a future goal or aspiration.
- Sensual Massage: Take turns giving each other sensual massages. Use touch, scent, and sound to create a relaxing and sensual experience for your partner.
- Intuitive Drawing: Sit facing each other with a piece of paper and a pen. Take turns drawing lines and shapes without thinking, allowing your intuition to guide you. Afterward, discuss what you created and what it means to you.
- Mirror Meditation: Sit facing each other and close your eyes. Take a few deep breaths and then open your eyes and gaze into your partner's eyes. Allow your breathing to sync up and focus on being fully present in the moment.
- Gratitude Exercise: Take turns expressing gratitude to each other. List things you appreciate about your partner and why.
- Cuddle Meditation: Lie down facing each other and cuddle. Take turns leading a meditation, either by guiding your partner through a visualization or simply focusing on your breath together.
- Body Scan Meditation: Lie down or sit comfortably with your partner and take turns leading a body scan meditation. Start at the top of your head and work your way down to your toes, bringing attention to each part of your body.
- Partner Yoga: Practice yoga together, either by taking a partner yoga class or following along with a partner yoga video. Partner yoga can be a great way to connect physically and emotionally.
- Mindful Walking: Take a walk together and practice being fully present in the moment. Notice the sights, sounds, and smells around you, and focus on walking in sync with each other.

- Active Listening: Sit facing each other and take turns speaking while the other partner listens actively. Focus on being present and fully engaged in the conversation.
- Mirror Exercise: Stand facing each other and mirror each other's movements. One person leads, and the other follows. Switch roles after a few minutes.
- Dancing: Put on some music and dance together. Focus on moving your bodies in sync and connecting with each other through movement.

The key to these embodiment exercises is to be fully present with each other and open to exploring different aspects of your relationship. It can be a great way to build intimacy, trust and connection, by being mindful and intentional with your time together, you can deepen your connection and strengthen your bond, but they can also bring up emotions and vulnerabilities.

Take the time to be fully present with each other and enjoy the experience. Be gentle with each other and take breaks as needed. If you have any concerns or discomfort, be sure to communicate openly and honestly with your partner.

Embodiment heals, in a delicate, compassionate, yet in a profound way, the wounds of the past and helps us to experience infinite love and closeness. It not only teaches us how to be great lovers but also how to be great healers for one another.

Love develops and opens the heart when we attain states of presence, energy flow, calm, harmony, and connection. Spiritual and sexual practices and rituals work together to create the conditions for love to thrive and survive.

To cultivate true love and passion in our relationship, we first need to develop a deep connection with our own body. Embodiment offers us methods for not just improving your relationship with ourselves, marriage/partnership, but also for strengthening the relationships with your children, extended family, and coworkers. By spending time each day practicing the techniques, we can gradually become more aware of our bodies and learn to inhabit them in a new way.

Make sure you feel the love that you are seeking from others within you first and let your heart guide you on your journey. When you are authentic and honest with yourself, you are closer to being truly happy. Remember, your body understands what it is talking about, and it is essential not to let yourself become disconnected from it.

Mindful Undressing Practice: Embodied Awareness for Intimacy and Connection

Undressing with mindfulness is a powerful exercise that can increase your intimate awareness and help you connect more deeply with your body, mind, and spirit. Whether you're doing it alone or with a partner, this exercise can be a beautiful and empowering experience.

If you're doing this exercise alone, find a quiet, private space where you feel comfortable and at ease. You can use a big mirror to see your full body, light some candles, and create a safe and loving atmosphere. Before you begin, take a few deep breaths, and ground yourself in the present moment. You might also want to take a moment to set an intention for the practice, such as self-love, self-acceptance, or deepening your connection to your body.

Start by touching yourself from head to toe on the outside of your clothes. Take your time and be mindful of the sensations you feel and the movements you make. Focus on the movements and sensations you may express with different intensities of touches. Then slowly undress yourself, savoring each moment of touch and intimacy. As your clothes come off, take the opportunity to touch without being touched, to look without being seen, and to explore every inch of your body.

Ask yourself questions like, "What do I see, hear, touch, taste, and smell right now?" and "What is happening in my body? What am I aware of?" Pay attention to how your emotions show up in your body sensations, and notice how your posture, breath, sensations, thoughts, and feelings change throughout the experience. Reflect on how you feel about yourself and your body. Be kind to yourself, and allow yourself to be curious without making assumptions or jumping to conclusions.

If you're doing this exercise with a partner, start by taking a few deep breaths together and grounding yourselves in the present moment. Take a moment to appreciate each other's bodies and express your love and gratitude. Begin by touching your partner from head to toe on the outside of their clothes. Take your time and be mindful of the sensations you feel and the movements you make. When you're ready, slowly undress your partner, savoring each moment of touch and intimacy.

As your partner's clothes come off, take the opportunity to touch without being touched, to look without being seen, and to explore every inch of their body. Ask yourself questions like, "What do I see, hear, touch, taste, and smell right now?" and "What is happening in my body? What am I aware of?" Pay attention to how your emotions show up in your body sensations, and notice how your posture, breath, sensations, thoughts, and feelings change throughout the experience. Reflect on how you feel about your partner and the two of you together.

Be kind to yourself and your partner and allow yourselves to be curious without making assumptions or jumping to conclusions. When you're finished, switch roles so you can both have your own mindfulness undressing experience. Take a moment to express your gratitude and love for each other, and reflect on how this practice can help deepen your connection and intimacy.

Remember, this exercise is about cultivating a deeper sense of awareness and connection with your body and your partner, not about achieving a certain outcome. Approach it with an open mind and an open heart, and allow yourself to be fully present in each moment. With practice, you can use this exercise to deepen your connection to yourself and your partner and enhance your intimate experiences.

Love and Connection Embodiment Meditation

Our meditation journey will help you to set up space for a powerful day or evening filled with personal presence so you can fully embody the energies of love and connection. Let's get started.

Find a comfortable position, minimizing distractions as best you can. You can choose to sit down with your back straight or lie down. Take a moment to stretch your body slowly and carefully. Gently close your eyes as we begin. Take a moment to settle into this space, leaving behind the distractions of the day.

As you do, become aware of your breath. Take a deep breath in, feeling your lungs expand, and release it fully. Follow the breath as it flows in and out of your body. Allow it to feel natural and easy. Don't try to force or regulate the breath in any way; simply let it flow naturally on its own. As you exhale, release any tension, letting go of any thoughts that don't serve you in this moment.

Inhale deeply, drawing in the limitless power of the universe. Feel the energy infuse your being, awakening the divine spark within you. Exhale slowly, releasing all doubts and limitations that have held you back. Now, shift your attention to your own body. Begin to scan your body, noticing any areas of tension or discomfort.

As you become aware of these areas, imagine them being wrapped in a warm, healing energy – much like the feeling around your heart. As you continue this scan, focus on parts of your body that you genuinely appreciate. These could be things you like about your appearance or qualities you admire in yourself. Maybe it's the strength and flexibility of your muscles, the gracefulness of your movements.

Consider how your body enables you to experience the world, the unique way your body carries you through each day. While concentrating on these areas, let yourself feel a sense of love and thankfulness for your body. Picture the warm, nurturing energy you've been building up flowing into these places, filling them with even more love and appreciation.

Now, bring to mind an image of yourself at your happiest and most fulfilled moment. Imagine embodying this version of yourself, glowing with happiness and confidence. Try to sense this joy and confidence in your body, letting it bring you a feeling of peace and satisfaction. Move on to deepening your connections. Your connections with your body, your mind, your soul and your higher self.

Envision a golden light surrounding your heart, representing the love and connection within you. See this light growing, spreading from your heart, filling your whole body and the space around you. While you focus on this light, repeat these affirmations silently: "I am full of love. I am connected to all living things. I am worthy of love and connection.

Now, remember a time when you felt deeply loved and connected. This could be a memory of a person, a place, or an experience. Try to bring this memory to life by using your senses – see the colours, feel the textures, hear the sounds. Let yourself be completely present in this moment. While you hold onto this memory, imagine its energy flowing into your body, filling you up with even more love and connection.

Allow yourself to fully feel this loving sensation, knowing you can access it whenever you need. Feel this memory spreading throughout your entire being, filling you with warmth and positivity. Imagine this feeling expanding outward from your heart, surrounding your body and space in a golden light.

Visualize yourself surrounded by a circle of people or beings you feel a strong connection with. Picture yourself holding hands with them, feeling the flow of love and connection moving freely between you all. Take a moment to embrace the strength of this bond, knowing you are never alone and always connected to the universe.

Allow yourself to fully immerse in the profound feeling that you have created within yourself. As you visualize this radiant feeling, imagine it expanding outwards and connecting you with others and the world around you. Take a moment to embrace this sensation and remain present with it for as long as you desire.

Observe any shifts or changes in your body and emotions as you let this feeling fill you up. Remember, when you fully embody love, you are embracing yourself and extending that love outward to the world. This creates a ripple effect of transformative power that has the potential to inspire and empower others.

This flame of love ignites positive change that extends far beyond ourselves, fostering a more compassionate, empathetic, and connected world. Love transcends boundaries and has the power to transform and create amazing opportunities for personal and spiritual growth.

So, remember how to bring yourself to this beautiful embodiment place and let your love radiate and be the catalyst for transformative change. You are a powerful creator, here to bring forth miracles for your highest good and the greater good. Embrace the power within you, for it knows no bounds.

Inhale once more, igniting the passion of your dreams. Exhale, releasing any remnants of doubt. You are ready, empowered, and aligned with the cosmic forces. Embrace this journey, for it is yours to shape and inspire.

When you're ready to bring the meditation to a close, take a few deep breaths, inhaling through your nose and exhaling through your mouth, allowing each breath to help you return to the present moment. Wiggle your toes, gently stretch your body, take your time and when you feel ready, open your eyes and take a moment to notice any shifts or changes in how you feel.

Reflect on the tranquility you've cultivated, and thank yourself for this time of mindfulness, presence and self-care.

NOTE: This meditation is available on my YouTube channel" @MarcelaOnyx".

What beliefs do I hold about my body that are limiting my ability to feel confident and empowered?

How can I deepen my awareness of my body's sensations and signals, and respond to them in a more intuitive and self-compassionate way?

What steps can I take to prioritize my physical and emotional well-being in my daily routine and adopt practices that support my mind-body connection and overall health?

How can I create a positive and empowering relationship with my body despite societal norms and expectations?

How can I shift negative self-talk and replace it with affirming messages that support self-love and body positivity?

How can I cultivate appreciation and respect for my body and its ability to nourish and support me?

What are my relationship needs, and how can I communicate them assertively and effectively with my partner?

How does it feel in my body when my needs are met, and what actions can I take to ensure that my needs are prioritized and respected in my relationships?

How can I explore and define "making love" and "great sex" for myself, and prioritize my pleasure and satisfaction in my sexual relationships?

What does a fulfilling sexual experience look like for me, and how can I communicate my needs and desires to my partner confidently and empowered?

How can I cultivate a deeper awareness and appreciation of my body's responses and sensations during intimacy, and communicate my needs and desires to my partner in a confident and empowered way?

How does my body respond to the visualizations and affirmations used in love and connection embodiment meditation? Am I able to feel the energy of love and connection flowing through my body? What shifts do I notice in my posture, breath, sensations, thoughts, and feelings during this practice?

How can I integrate the experiences and insights gained from these practices into my daily life? How might they enhance my overall well-being, self-acceptance, and ability to connect with others?

My body is an incredible machine that carries me through life, and I am grateful for my body, for its strength and resilience and for all the experiences it allows me to have in this world. I radiate confidence and sexiness, honouring my body with love and care. Every time I look in the mirror, I see a beautiful, happy person looking back at me, and I am in love with the person I am becoming.

I am my biggest cheerleader, celebrating my accomplishments and admiring the qualities that make me unique. I have everything I need within me. When I am present in my body, breathing and relaxing, I tap into my inner power and embrace the fullness of my sexuality.

CHAPTER 8

Spicing Up and Keeping the Flame

You have awakened. You have embraced your vulnerability and owned your sexuality! Congratulations! I could not be more thrilled! But what comes next? How do you maintain, nurture, and cultivate the vulnerability and intimacy that is arisen after such a long journey?

After awakening, we are often flooded with a sense of joy, love, and freedom. We may also experience a heightened sense of awareness and intuition. All of these are positive signs that we are on the right track. But if we are not careful, it is easy to let the spark fade when dealing with the stresses of daily life. It is a fact that as we age it is common to feel changes in all aspects of our life and in some cases it can also include a decline in sexual frequency.

According to the 2018 General Social Survey's data on about 660 married people who shared details about how often they had sex in the past year:

- ➤ 25% had sex once a week.
- ➤ 16% had sex two to three times per week.
- ➤ 5% had sex four or more times per week.
- ➤ 17% had sex once a month.
- ➤ 19% had sex two to three times per month.
- ➤ 10% hadn't had sex in the past year.
- ➤ 7% had sex about once or twice in the past year.

Everyone is different. If you and your partner are content with not having sex or having it whenever you both feel like it because it is a common choice, you are entitled not to feel sexual.

There are a lot of people who might go through a period without having sex, or who don't have desire yet are in a very happy and stable and loving relationship.

Love, acceptance, respect, admiration, gratitude, great communication, laughter, partnership, and care are also very pleasurable.

Sometimes it is important to recognize when the relationship would benefit from giving your partner space and having your space, as individuals we also need our own time for self-care, to do whatever we like, or even spend time alone enjoying the silence of our home, or travelling, or hanging out with our family and friends. Let both breathe and miss each other, have new things to share about your time apart, and also plan something to look forward to doing together.

When it comes to keeping the spark alive, why not try learning something new together? It does not have to be something big—it could be a new hobby, dance, arts, sport, or language… Learning something new as a couple can help keep things fresh and fun. It helps break through any mental blocks or boredom that you may have. For example, if you are both into yoga, why not try some new poses in the bedroom? It also takes away any pressure of having to perform—you can focus on enjoying each other's company and learning together. Plus, it adds an extra layer of intimacy to your relationship as you share new experiences and support each other in this journey.

Bringing some surprise and adventure into your lives is a wonderful way to spice things up and help you both keep the excitement that was there in the beginning.

What memories do you have from the beginning of your relationship that makes you smile?

I will share two with you. My partner once travelled one hour to leave roses in my car parked at the gym. It looked like anonymous roses from a secret admirer, as there were no cards. I passed some of them onto another car to make someone else smile. He only acknowledged that it was him two days later when he gave me the rest of the roses confessing that he was the admirer. He always demonstrates so much respect for my beloved late husband, has lots of patience and is very caring when I have my moments of grief.

It is little gestures that count, the values that we have seen in our partners, how safe and connected we feel, the things we do that give each other reassurance that we have met the right person that can make us smile, feel loved and in a harmonious and happy relationship.

It is essential to maintain the energy created at the beginning of any meaningful relationship. This includes the energy generated during your awakening to vulnerability and sexuality. Approach it with authenticity, romance, passion, trust, consent, love and acceptance. Make a commitment to be fully present in your relationship rather than seeking fulfillment solely from it.

Do you remember what it felt like to fall in love? When falling in love, we make efforts, we are in this crazy, awesome biochemistry of lust and interest to get to know each other, and we plan dates we seduce each other, give compliments, and feel appreciated.

I am glad that you now remember what matters most to you when you had fallen in love, so whatever you choose to do, make sure it's something that:

- ✓ Allows plenty of quality time.
- ✓ It has your partner's consent (unless it's a pleasant surprise or involves something you had previously discussed in the past).
- ✓ Does not involve constant interruptions from work or everyday life distractions.

This means taking the time to spice your relationship and keep it alive so that the thrill of a new flame does not fade. It is all about getting out of the routine and having fun.

I would love to share some fool proof (and fun!) ways to do just that in this chapter.

- Organize a home spa day and give each other a full body massage; massages are a great way to relax and get to know each other better; add essential oils for an extra sensual touch. If you are feeling creative, use massage candles or aromatic massage oil. Practice breathing exercises or yoga positions, and prepare a light meal. The idea is to spend quality time, create connection and intimacy, be present to each other, give and receive and have fun.

- Give tight hugs and long kisses more often. Hugs naturally put a person in a good headspace, making them feel relaxed and connected to you. Kissing releases oxytocin (the so-called "love hormone"), a chemical that increases feelings of empathy and connection to your partner. In addition, kissing can help create the right atmosphere for intimacy in moments where it just feels like you are "going through the motions".

- Book to stay in a fancy hotel and get breakfast in bed. Enjoy lounging, talking, singing (I love it), and enjoying each other's company (phones off unless you expect an important call).

- If you cannot be together in person, use technology to schedule regular virtual coffee, lunch, and dates, or send each other regular love notes or funny memes throughout the day. Sexting can be a fun way to keep things spicy, and there are even apps designed specifically for couples that can help you share fantasies and connect on a deeper level.

- Challenge each other to do something you have never done together or do not like or even have not tried, but your partner shows some interest. Trust each other to teach and explore together, getting out of each other comfort zone. You may be surprised and enjoy the outcome.

- Remind each other how important you are to each other, do it with appreciation and gratitude. You can even add gratitude into your routine and, as a practice, share a moment of gratitude for things that happened during your day. Most people do not even know how empowering this can be in a relationship.

- Revisit places that remind both of you of your favorite memories together.
- Have a romantic picnic or a hot air balloon with a champagne experience.
- Grab blankets and pillows and go stargazing.
- Go for a hike, bike ride, take a nature walk or explore unfamiliar places.
- Book a holiday with an all-inclusive resort, explore places to visit and make the most of the experience as a couple.
- Try new recipes from around the world and learn about the culture
- Create your Sex playlist while having a glass of wine, cocktails or your favorite drink, dance and be creative. Try teasing strip techniques for each other…
- Create a vision board for your future

Give a Gift to Your Partner That Will Keep Your Intimacy Strong

Think outside the box here and get each other something special. Perhaps a new sex toy that you can both use, something that adds excitement to your bedroom and introduces some new fun. A new stocking or outfit or a game designed to bring out your flirtatious side. What matters most is an intimate gift from the heart or a thoughtful gesture. And if all else fails, why not surprise each other with an evening of passion and pleasure? This works for any budget!

Incorporate Role-Play and Fantasies

Adding a little spice to your sex life is a great way to keep your relationship from becoming too static. One of the best ways to do this is to use role-play and fantasies. Try setting up a scene, talking in character, and playing out different scenarios.

Sex toys can also add an extra level of excitement to your sex life and can help you explore new sexual experiences with your partner. It is always essential that both in a relationship feel that they are safe and secure in their sex lives. There are a wide variety of sex toys available on the market, so do your research to find the right one for you and your partner and communicate about it.

If unsure where to start, you can always consult a sex toy expert to find the perfect toys or accessories for you and your partner.

Role-play with costumes and become someone else for the night. Lingerie can be fabulous for this or any outfit you like - even a change of clothes can do the trick.

There are no fundamental rules - dive in and have fun! Please make a list of your fantasies and try them out over time. By engaging with each other in this way, you will find that it can help to enhance and deepen your connection, remove any fear of judgment, and allow you both to explore and discover new things about one another.

Make the Most Out of What You Have at Home

Have you ever watched a movie and found yourself inspired to recreate scenes from it in your bedroom? Making the most out of what you have at home is a way to keep the spark alive.

From something as simple as lighting a few candles and buying sexy lingerie to investing in a high-quality set of silk sheets, there are tons of options available that will not break the bank. You could also play sexy music, spray a scent that turns you both on or use creative props such as blindfolds and restraints during sex.

Find New Ways to Communicate

Consider writing love letters, poems, or even text messages during the day to let your partner know you are thinking of them. Try to create a secret language between you and your partner by making up your own words for certain concepts or situations. This can be an incredibly fun way to express yourselves and keep the spark alive between you two.

That is not all. I have more suggestions for you.

Talk dirty: Start by sending your partner a dirty text message or something that you "Want To" it can be anything you are enthusiastic about or looking forward to exploring. Try whispering something naughty in their ear when you're in public. Or maybe start your text with "Willing To", which means you are open to trying something new that you do not know if you will like, but you are willing to explore it. The key is to be creative and to let your imagination run wild.

Tantric/sacred sex: Take classes on Tantra or other religious paths that will allow you to experience a deeper level of intimacy and a new level of mind, body, and spirit connection with your lover.

Spontaneous quickie: At any time is exciting and boosts your energy and mood levels throughout the day.

Play a sexy game: Couples who play together stay together. There are so many options, and some you can even find as online resources and have fun. It's up to be creative and have some fun: Punishment/Rewards Play, Cross-Dressing (Gender Play), Interrog Scenes, Sexopoly, Strip poker, Blindfold and restraint, The fantasy box, Couples twister game, and Temperature play. If you have not tried yet, here are a few ideas to get you started.

Try new positions: Try something new and have fun with it! Why not consider exploring Kama sutra? Choose a few positions that you never tried before and incorporate them during the foreplay as a teaser only. By getting a bit creative, you could find positions that feel more comfortable than others and offer more pleasure. You could also try a position like the spooning position, which allows both partners to be close together and comfortable while having intimate contact. Another idea is to use a sex pillow or wedge that can help create different angles and make certain positions easier to get into—the bonus being less strain on your body.

Start keeping a "Naughty Journal": Whether you're single or in a relationship, this can be an incredibly helpful tool for creating more variety in your sex life and awakening your naughty, kinky and or BDSM (Bondage, Discipline, Sadism, Masochism) and creative side. And sometimes, it's also about feeling free to explore new things on your own time and without worrying about judgment from others.

The key here is not worrying about what other people think—you simply write down what may turn you on.

Visit erotic destinations: This could mean a sex-themed resort, an adult-only cruise, or even a visit to a local sex shop. When you visit one of these places, the goal is to have fun, explore new things together, and reignite your passion for each other.

Create a Sensation Play Mood: Setting the mood for an intimate evening never gets old, and the atmosphere can often help set the tone for a hot and steamy evening. Explore each other senses with long, slow touches. Touch is known to produce high pleasure or orgasm. Touch their entire body, use your fingertips, feathers, fur, chains and other various objects. You can even try touch combined with meditation, visualisation, or breathwork.

Add light bondage: Don't let the word "bondage" intimidate you — you don't have to go full-on Fifty Shades of Gray or 365 days right away. Start small and work your way up.

Invest in simple restraints, like velvet scarves, and tease each other with them during foreplay. Introduce blindfolds, which can prevent your partner from anticipating what comes next, creating suspense and a psychology of anticipation. Then, create a safe word or signal so both of you feel comfortable stopping anytime. Or switch up roles by playing mistress/master/dominant.

But remember, safety comes first! Be sure to read up on safe practices around bondage, and never do anything that makes you or your partner uncomfortable.

Schedule date nights: Have something special to look forward to doing together at least once a month; regular date nights can do wonders for your relationship, especially if you both have your mobiles switched off. It allows you and your partner to connect, catch up on recent events, and enjoy each other's company without the distraction of kids or work. Plus, spending quality time together outside the bedroom can build a strong connection that easily translates into increased passion and better sex.

Take a shower together: This is an easy one, but it's also the most fun. You can do it at home or in a hotel, and you'll have plenty of time to get clean and have some fun; maybe make it even more exciting by getting dirty by trying a playful body painting, condensed milk, juice fruits,   to make the shower experience even more fun. Just make out while you're getting cleaned up!

Watch an erotic movie together: Why not put on an erotic film and have some fun together? It's a great way to get things started and help you both in the mood. You don't even have to watch it all the way through—pop it in, get cosy together on the couch, and enjoy each other's company. You may even get inspired to take things to the next level.

Read erotica to each other: Pick a few hot passages from your favorite book or check out some steamy new erotica together. You may be surprised at how turned on you both get! Not only does it get you in the mood, but it can also be a fun way to learn about your partner's likes and dislikes.

I hope you have enjoyed this chapter as much as I did in writing it.

Don't Be Afraid to Try Something New!

It may just be the spark you need to keep things hot!

Spice up your relationship with yourself and your partner, keep the sexy flame burning and renew it any time you feel you would benefit from it, avoid routine, and don't let things get too stale. You are in control of your own intimate and sexual happiness.

Space for Self-Reflection

What are my deepest desires and fantasies when it comes to spicing up my sexual and intimate experiences?

How can I explore and experiment with playfulness in my sexual experiences with my partner?

In what ways can I support and fulfil my partner's desires and needs while also honouring my own?

What are some creative ways I can maintain a sense of novelty and excitement in my sexual experiences with my long-term partner?

How can I prioritize my own pleasure and satisfaction while also ensuring that my partner's needs and desires are met?

What new experiences or techniques am I willing to try to bring more excitement to my sexual experiences with my partner?

How can I be more open to playfulness and experimentation in my sexual experiences with my partner?

What new facets of my sexuality and desires am I willing to explore and embrace?

How can I ensure that my sexual experiences are always consensual and respectful for both myself and my partner?

What barriers or challenges am I currently facing in maintaining a satisfying sexual relationship, and how can I overcome them?

Some couples or individuals like to have sexual goals like, for example, reconnecting with their partner, healing past wounds, overcoming sexual issues, and learning how they can improve their sexual skills. What are my sexual goals?

What steps can I take to reignite the passion and romance in my relationship, and how can I prevent complacency or boredom from setting in?

Write down your bucket list of things you want to do, pursue, explore, or places you want to visit that may spice up your intimate relationship with yourself (if you are single) or with your partner or even both if you love to also spend time with yourself and do the things that make you happy.

How do I prioritize quality time with my partner? How can I ensure that our time together is uninterrupted by work or everyday distractions? What steps can I take to create an environment conducive to connection, intimacy, and fun?

How do I currently express my love and appreciation for my partner? Are there additional ways I can show them how much they mean to me?

Make a twelve-month plan, including one special date with yourself or your partner. Where do you want to go? What do you want to do? What fantasies may you have in mind for those special date nights? Commit to it!

January

February

March

April

May

June

July

August

September

October

November

December

Space for Self-Reflection & Celebration

This is It!

Our journey together in this book is coming to an end, and it has been my greatest pleasure welcoming and walking with you from page one. While this is your journey to walk, it's possible and normal to feel overwhelmed or need help. You might also need someone to talk and walk you through some related areas of your life. Feel free to reach out to me if you need help with any part. I am just a contact away!

For now, it's **time to celebrate your growth**.

Complete any of the previous "Space for Self-Reflection" sections that you may have missed.

Reflect on your growth journey and write about what you have learned about yourself.

Identify the most exciting parts of your growth journey.

Consider how your growth will bring better connections to your life.

Reflect on how you see an intimate relationship with yourself and your partner in the future.

What have you learned about yourself throughout your growth journey? How has self-discovery shaped your understanding of who you are?

Think about the breakthroughs or accomplishments that brought you the most joy and satisfaction. How did they impact your personal growth?

My intimate life is a constant source of joy and inspiration, reminding me of the incredible richness that lies within me, waiting to be discovered. Through the power of my sexuality, I embrace each moment with excitement and gratitude, free to choose how and when I express my desires and needs. Every intimate encounter is an opportunity to explore and celebrate the beauty and wonder of my existence, deepening my connection to myself and others. With an open heart and a courageous spirit, I welcome the journey ahead, eager to discover the full range of my erotic power and experience the profound fulfillment that comes with it.

Conclusion

Congratulations on completing the transformative journey of self-discovery and personal growth in "Awaken to Embrace Vulnerability and Sexuality" book! You have come a long way and should be proud of yourself.

We embarked on a transformative journey of self-discovery and personal growth. We learned to embrace vulnerability as a strength that opened us up to new experiences and opportunities for growth. We set healthy boundaries to create space for healthy relationships to flourish, and we awakened to the power of intimacy, emotional connection, and healing to strengthen our relationships. We also learned the essential role of self-love, compassion, and acceptance in embracing our unique sexuality and the importance of embodiment, creativity, and playfulness in keeping our relationships fulfilling and passionate. Through those chapters, we empowered ourselves to live our lives with authenticity, courage, passion, and purpose, while building fulfilling relationships with ourselves and others.

Now that you have gained new insights and tools for personal growth, it's time to put them into action! You are capable of creating positive change in your life, but it's important to be kind and patient with yourself. Remember that transformation is a journey, and it takes time to integrate new habits and ways of being. Trust the process and keep moving forward with self-compassion and determination.

If you wish to have more support in enhancing your relationship and intimate life, Feel free to connect with me whenever you're ready. Let's explore how we can work together and create a more fulfilling experience in your life and relationship.

I wish you all the best on your journey of self-discovery.

Enjoy the best intimate relationship with yourself and your partner.

Be you, be brave, be love!

I love you.

Marcela ♡nyx

EXCLUSIVE
Chapter

Healing Visibility

Heal the wounds of invisibility, embracing the power of vulnerability to grow andtransform.

Embrace your true essence, letting go of masks and revealing your authentic self.

Awaken to the importance of visibility, recognizing its impact on all aspects of life -personal, social, professional, and spiritual growth.

Liberate yourself from fear, doubt, uncertainty, past pain and traumas.

Illuminate the hidden parts of your identity, embracing self-awareness, self-acceptance, forgiveness and compassion.

Nurture meaningful connections, as visibility strengthens bonds and fosters empathy.

Grow in confidence and resilience, embracing visibility as a catalyst for positivechange.

Value your uniqueness and individuality and discover the essence of your being.

Illuminate the hidden aspects of your identity, embracing vulnerability as a path tohealing.

Shed the veils of self-doubt and fear, stepping into the light of your authenticity.

Ignite your passion for growth and transformation.

Break free from the chains of invisibility, empowering yourself to be seen and heard.

Inspire connections built on trust and understanding, forging meaningfulrelationships
Leverage your visibility to inspire others, creating a ripple effect of positive change.

Inquire within, cultivating introspection for profound self-discovery.

Transform your life, unlocking your full potential and purpose.

You hold the key to self-empowerment and ignite positive change in your life andothers.

We all appreciate when we are being acknowledged, accepted, and celebrated forour authentic selves. In a world where visibility extends far beyond the physical, it'seasy to get lost in the hustle and bustle of life – both online and offline. We oftenfind ourselves navigating the labyrinth of social media, career aspirations, andpersonal relationships, each demanding its share of our attention.

The truth is, that the glow of visibility often conceals an inner journey that's just asimpressive as their outward presence. Some individuals naturally excel at grabbingattention, like confidently presenting their ideas in a boardroom or captivating anonline audience effortlessly. However, we frequently overlook the personal voyagemany have embarked upon – a path of self-acceptance, resilience, and continuousgrowth. People who stand out may have invested countless hours in self-reflection,faced their own doubts and fears, and embarked on a quest to uncover theirauthentic selves.

Visibility is a spectrum that spans various aspects of our lives. From the personalrealm, where we build relationships and explore our passions, to the professionalarena, where we chase our ambitions, the friendships we nurture, the conversationswe engage in, and the moments we share – all contribute to this spectrum.

The influence of culture and society on our self-perception is undeniable. Elementssuch as gender, race, sexuality, and abilities add complex and detailed aspects to ourtrue experiences and path in life. Every interaction, whether big or small, holds thepotential to impact our self-esteem, shape our sense of belonging, and influence ouroverall well-being. This importance lies in being emotionally, mentally, and spirituallypresent.

This is why it's crucial to cultivate self-awareness, embark on a journey of self-discovery, express ourselves authentically, show self-compassion, and foster healingand growth. By delving into the depths of our minds, understanding our strengths,values, and passions, and acknowledging our triggers, past pains, traumas, fears, andaspirations, we can embrace vulnerability as a gateway to growth while confidentlyexpressing our true selves.

Being visible means embracing our uniqueness and sharing our ideas and opinionswith authenticity and courage. It is not driven by seeking validation or approval;Worthiness comes from within.

For those of us who lean towards being reserved and private, embracing visibility canevoke a wide array of emotions. It's natural to feel awkward, uncomfortable, andeven exhausted when we put ourselves out there.

In social environments, engaging with others and initiating conversations may initiallyfeel challenging, particularly if we cherish our moments of solitude and introspection.Advocating for our accomplishments in professional settings can be daunting, as wefear coming across as boastful or insincere. Consistently sharing our artistic work canbe tiring for creative people, especially when we value our privacy.

Opening up emotionally in personal relationships can be uncomfortable for introvertswho hold their private space dear. And even when presented with leadershipopportunities, some of us may feel a bit hesitant, as we prefer to lead by examplerather than seeking the limelight.

Embracing visibility doesn't mean changing who we are at our core; it meansallowing the world to see the unique and remarkable qualities that make us who weare.

Feeling invisible or unnoticed can have both perceived benefits and potentialdrawbacks. On one hand, it may provide individuals with a sense of freedom, lesspressure, and the opportunity for self-reflection. They may find it easier to observeand learn from others, act authentically, and explore their creativity without fear ofjudgment. Additionally, being unnoticed might alleviate social pressure, allow forpersonal growth, and offer the chance to assess situations before activelyparticipating. Moreover, feeling invisible can lead individuals to develop resilienceand self-reliance and, in some cases, avoid unwanted attention or conflicts.

However, prolonged feelings of invisibility can also lead to isolation and negativeimpacts on mental and emotional well-being. While enjoying moments of privacy andfreedom can be beneficial, finding a balance between being unseen and forminggenuine connections with others is crucial for fostering healthy relationships andoverall life satisfaction. It's essential to stay mindful of how feeling invisible may affectone's well-being and seek support and connection when needed.

Many of us have felt unseen and unnoticed during challenging times, particularly in aworld where societal norms, biases, or exclusionary practices may contribute to thissense of invisibility. This experience of being overlooked can lead to a range ofnegative effects on individuals, impacting them emotionally and in their relationships. These consequences encompass emotional distress, diminished self-esteem,withdrawal from social and work-related engagements, decreased motivation,strained interpersonal connections, communication difficulties, reduced productivity,and potential implications for mental well-being.

Furthermore, this feeling of invisibility can permeate various aspects of life,potentially diminishing overall fulfilment and happiness. It may become necessary forindividuals to seek guidance in finding purpose and significance within theirinteractions and pursuits. Each of us carries our own unique stories, some filled withjoy and others marked by pain and trauma. These painful experiences can takedifferent forms, whether it's the inability to meet basic human needs, enduringphysical or emotional abuse, facing natural disasters, or confronting life-alteringevents that evoke feelings of pain, fear, and shame. These emotions shape ourthoughts, words, behaviours, and ultimately influence our presence – whether in ourpersonal lives or the wider world.

Perhaps you are someone like me who feels very comfortable speaking on stage, intheaters, and on camera, but it has not always been this way. I also know what itmeans to hide – and I'm not talking about playing hide and seek. I mean the kind ofhiding where you feel the fear and choose not to do it anyway, where you want to beinvisible. We tend to do it for many different reasons and sometimes even adoptcoping mechanisms to protect ourselves, even though some of them may not behealthy.

Throughout my journey to heal my own visibility wounds, I've gained valuableinsights into the purpose each one has served and how I've grown from theseexperiences. This inspiration led me to write this chapter and made me realize that Icould even write an entire book in the future.

The most common fears linked to visibility include the fear of betrayal, ridicule,vulnerability, comparison, success, fear of change, uncertainty, punishment,unwanted attention, loss of privacy, criticism, rejection, boundary avoidance, andeven a lack of skills or confidence in sales or using technology (Tech-Insecurity). Manytools exist for healing, but one highly effective approach, drawn from both mypersonal experience and work with clients, is Medical Intuitive healing. During thesesessions, I intuitively identify the most relevant blockages for the healing process andestablish a connection between the client and their wounded selves, addressing thepain or trauma they wish to discuss. This enables deeper healing beyond the impactsof affirmations, reframing, and meditation. While various methods can be employed,this approach demonstrates a more enduring impact, resulting in a profound sense ofhealing and inner peace.

Reflect and Explore: Gaining Deeper Self-Awareness

Navigating Your Visibility Comfort Zone

Use these questions to become more aware of your comfort with being visible invarious aspects of life. Take your time and answer thoughtfully:

Relationships: Authentic Expression in Connections

Have you hesitated to express your true feelings and thoughts in relationships due tothe fear of judgment? Write down instances when you've avoided expressing yourselfand note how it made you feel or what triggered this hesitation.

Career: Shining a Light on Your Achievements

Do you find yourself avoiding opportunities to showcase your skills andaccomplishments at work because of worries about negative feedback? Jot downspecific situations where you held back and describe your emotions or triggersassociated with those moments.

Social Environments: Embracing Social Interaction

Are you uncomfortable initiating conversations or making connections in socialgatherings? Write about times when you avoided social interactions and describe thesensations or thoughts that emerged.

Personal Growth: Embracing Your Creative Potential

Does the fear of rejection or lack of recognition hold you back from pursuing yourpassions or sharing your creative work? Note down instances where you hesitated toshowcase your talents and detail the feelings or factors that contributed to thishesitation.

Emotional Expression: Navigating Vulnerability

Do you face challenges in opening up emotionally and being vulnerable with others?Write about situations where you held back your emotions and describe theemotions or fears that prevented you from expressing yourself.

Leadership: Leading with Authenticity

Do you avoid taking on leadership roles or guiding others due to concerns abouthow you might be perceived? Describe moments when you hesitated to step into aleadership position and note the triggers or thoughts behind this hesitation.

Public Speaking: Speaking Your Truth

Do you experience anxiety or self-doubt when faced with public speaking orpresenting? Write about specific instances when you felt anxious and describe theemotions or thoughts that contributed to your unease.

Self-Promotion: Celebrating Your Worth

Is promoting yourself or your business difficult for you due to fears of being seen asself-centered or arrogant? Note down situations where you hesitated to self-promoteand describe the feelings or concerns that influenced your decision.

Risk-Taking: Embracing New Opportunities

Does the fear of failure or the unknown prevent you from embracing newopportunities or taking risks? Write about instances when you avoided stepping outof your comfort zone and detail the emotions or worries that held you back.

Online Presence: Authenticity in the Digital World

Have you avoided sharing personal stories or videos online due to concerns abouthow strangers might respond? Describe moments when you held back from onlineexpression and note the triggers or apprehensions that played a role.

Boundaries: Asserting Your Authenticity

Does the fear of potential conflicts or disagreements stop you from settingboundaries and asserting your needs? Write about situations where you struggled toestablish boundaries and describe the emotions or reasons behind your hesitation.

Well Done on Taking the Time

Well done on taking the time to complete the previous exercise. Reflecting on yourcomfort with visibility in various areas of your life is an important step towardunderstanding your own challenges and strengths.

Exploring Archetypes: Connecting with Your Patterns

Perhaps you will find a connection with one or more of the archetypes below, just as Idid while I was on my inner journey to address past pain and traumas. I hopeexploring these archetypes will be as insightful for you as it was for me: each oneembodies distinct traits and tendencies. By examining these archetypes, we gainvaluable insights into different patterns of behavior and thought. It's a chance toexplore how these archetypes manifest in various aspects of our life.

The Hermit: Embracing Solitude

The Hermit represents someone who cherishes solitude and prefers to keep adistance from others. They guard their unique ideas and creations, often stemmingfrom past experiences where they faced ridicule or disapproval. These instances leftthem feeling embarrassed and criticized when they attempted to showcase theirwork. Consequently, they retreat into secrecy, missing out on opportunities to makea significant impact. Struggling with self-doubt and fearing judgment, they believetheir talents are inadequate and worry about the opinions of others. This mindsetconfines them to a cycle of self-imposed invisibility, preventing them from fullyexpressing their creativity and sharing their gifts with the world.

The Perfectionist: Pursuit of Flawlessness

The Perfectionist grapples with a persistent fear of imperfection. This anxietycompels them to withhold their work until it reaches an unrealistic standard offlawlessness. Their desire to avoid criticism or failure leads to overexertion andhesitancy in revealing their creations. Rooted in childhood experiences of inadequacy and harsh feedback, they associate self-worth with achieving perfection. This internalstruggle causes them to delay and question their abilities, inhibiting the full utilizationof their talents and potential. Overcoming this hurdle requires dismantling the notionof perfection and embracing the authentic expression of their creativity.

The Martyr: Sacrificing Self for Others

The Martyr places others' needs above their own, shying away from the spotlight toavoid appearing selfish. Childhood lessons of selflessness have ingrained a belief thatseeking recognition detracts from their role in supporting others. Consequently, theysuppress their aspirations and goals, neglecting their own talents. Their internalconflict centers around acknowledging their worth and navigating the balancebetween self-care and serving others. To break free from this cycle, they mustrecognize the importance of self-nurturing and value their contributions withoutundermining their achievements.

The Impostor: Battling Self-Doubt

The Impostor is plagued by self-doubt and a persistent feeling of unworthiness. Theyfear exposure as a fraud and anticipate that others will perceive them as inadequate.Past experiences of insufficient praise or validation fuel this insecurity, leading themto overcompensate by exerting extra effort and concealing perceived weaknesses.Their battle with feeling undeserving undermines their self-expression and preventsthem from fully embracing their capabilities. The path to growth involves challengingthese self-limiting beliefs and acknowledging that their value transcends externalvalidation.

The Rebel: Defying Conformity

The Rebel resists conformity and avoids visibility to preserve their unique identity.They fear that recognition may lead to compromising their individuality andconforming to societal norms. This resistance is rooted in past instances of feelingjudged or stifled for being authentic. This fear of losing their true self andapprehension of criticism compels them to remain in the shadows. Embracing theiruniqueness and overcoming the fear of judgment allows them to channel theircreativity and distinctiveness without compromising their identity.

The Avoider: Fear of Negative Judgment

The Avoider shies away from the spotlight due to a deep-seated fear of negativejudgment and criticism. Previous experiences of unpleasant reactions or hurtfulencounters while being noticed reinforce this aversion. They believe that stayinghidden shields them from potential harm, resulting in missed opportunities forgrowth and self-expression. Overcoming this challenge entails confronting thesefears, gradually stepping into the spotlight, and realizing that avoidance limits theirpotential.

The Caretaker: Nurturing Others, Neglecting Self

The Caretaker prioritizes others' needs and downplays their own accomplishments toavoid seeming self-centered. Rooted in a learned behavior of selflessness, theyassociate seeking recognition with selfishness and focus on nurturing and supportingothers. Their internal conflict lies in reconciling their desire for self-expression withthe fear of appearing egotistical. Shifting this perspective involves recognizing thatself-advocacy is essential for holistic well-being and balanced relationships.

The Procrastinator: Fear of Judgment and Failure

The Procrastinator grapples with fear of judgment and failure, leading to perpetualpostponement of sharing their work. This fear stifles their progress and creativity,rooted in a belief that their efforts will not meet expectations. They worry aboutexposing themselves to potential criticism and therefore avoid showcasing theircreations. Overcoming this obstacle involves challenging self-doubt, reframing failureas a stepping stone, and taking courageous steps towards visibility.

The Dreamer: Hesitation in Pursuing Dreams

The Dreamer possesses grand aspirations but hesitates to share them, fearingrejection and pressure. Their dreams remain confined to their thoughts due toconcerns about others' reactions and a lack of confidence in their own capabilities.The fear of vulnerability and potential failure hinders them from pursuingopportunities that could lead to success. Overcoming this challenge necessitatesembracing vulnerability, acknowledging that failure is part of the journey, and takingsteps towards realizing their dreams.

The People Pleaser: Seeking Approval

The People Pleaser avoids visibility out of a fear of disappointing others and invitingnegative judgment. Driven by a strong desire to please and avoid conflict, theysuppress their individuality and achievements. Childhood experiences of seekingapproval and avoiding displeasure contribute to this fear of being perceived asselfish or attention-seeking. This perpetual pattern prevents them from fullyexpressing their talents and realizing their potential.

The Self-Saboteur: Undermining Self-Worth

The Self-Saboteur unwittingly obstructs their progress and visibility due to deep-rooted feelings of unworthiness. Past failures and a lack of self-trust lead them toundermine their own efforts, fearing both success and failure. This fear-drivenbehavior stems from a belief that they don't deserve recognition and the worry thatsuccess could reveal their perceived inadequacies. Overcoming this cycle requiresconfronting these self-sabotaging tendencies, nurturing self-compassion, andfostering a sense of self-worth.

The Envious Observer: Overcoming Comparison

The Envious Observer watches others' achievements with a sense of inferiority,feeling incapable of attaining similar success. This comparison-driven perspectivediminishes their self-esteem and hinders them from showcasing their own talents.Rooted in a lack of self-assurance, they avoid visibility to evade unfavorablecomparisons and maintain a sense of self-worth. Challenging this mindset involvesrecognizing their unique strengths and accomplishments, leading to a moreconfident and empowered expression of their abilities.

The Control Freak: Liberating from Fear

The Control Freak shies away from visibility due to an intense fear of unpredictabilityand a loss of control. They associate the spotlight with potential chaos anddiscomfort, stemming from past instances of feeling overwhelmed by unforeseencircumstances. Their need for control restrains them from taking risks and embracingthe unknown, trapping them in a cycle of avoidance. To break free, they mustcultivate a willingness to relinquish control, acknowledge their capacity to adapt, andopen themselves to new possibilities.

The Overwhelmed Perfectionist: Embracing Progress

The Overwhelmed Perfectionist grapples with a dual struggle of pursuing perfectionwhile feeling overwhelmed by the enormity of the task. Fear of failure and a desirefor flawlessness hinder them from sharing their work, as they battle the pressure tomeet impossibly high standards. This cycle of hesitation and striving for perfectionarises from past experiences of harsh critique or personal doubt. To transcend thischallenge, they must embrace imperfection, recognize the value of progress overperfection, and acknowledge their accomplishments along the way.

The Prover: Shifting Validation

The Prover seeks external validation as a measure of their worthiness and hesitates toexpress themselves without approval. Their reliance on others' praise stems frompast instances of feeling unnoticed or undervalued. This external validation-drivenapproach inhibits authentic self-expression, as they perceive their own value throughothers' eyes. Overcoming this challenge involves shifting the focus from externalvalidation to intrinsic self-worth, fostering self-confidence, and embracing self-expression for its inherent value.

The Hidden Genius: Unveiling Unique Talents

The Hidden Genius possesses exceptional skills but harbors reservations aboutshowcasing them. Fearing unwanted attention and pressure, they keep their talentsconcealed. This fear of exposure and potential judgment is rooted in pastexperiences of criticism or rejection related to their abilities. Overcoming this hurdle entails embracing vulnerability, recognizing the potential for positive impact, andboldly sharing their unique talents with the world.

The Fearful Artist: Embracing Artistic Expression

The Fearful Artist struggles to unveil their creative work due to apprehensions aboutcriticism and rejection. They withhold their art to avoid potential negative feedbackand maintain their emotional well-being. This fear-based behavior originates frompast experiences of criticism or lack of acceptance. To break free, they must cultivateself-confidence, embrace constructive feedback, and understand that their artisticexpression holds inherent value regardless of others' opinions.

The Comparison Trap: Reframing Self-Perception

The Comparison Trap ensnares individuals in a cycle of self-doubt, as they constantlymeasure themselves against others. This self-comparison fuels feelings ofinadequacy, dissuading them from showcasing their unique talents. Rooted in a lackof self-assurance, this fear of unfavorable comparison prevents them from steppinginto the spotlight. Overcoming this challenge necessitates focusing on theirindividual strengths, acknowledging personal growth, and reframing self-comparisonas an opportunity for self-improvement.

Navigating the Path to Authentic Visibility

We all face self-doubt and worry about what others think. However, when we allowfear to control us, we miss out on a full and genuine life. To shift our outlook, weneed to redirect negative thoughts and be kinder to ourselves. A helpful strategy isto ask ourselves, 'Is there any real proof for these fears?' Often, we'll discover thatour fears are merely assumptions, not facts.

By progressively exposing ourselves to situations that trigger fear and realizing thatour worst fears don't always materialize, we can cultivate resilience and confidence inour ability to handle criticism. The synergy of Healing Visibility and self-loveempowers us to explore our true selves, become stronger, and nurture greaterconfidence. This self-love also guides us in attracting positivity into our work and life.

Embrace self-love starting now, and you'll witness how it enriches your journey.

Being open and vulnerable can make it easier to face fear and be more visible. Thinkabout those brave people who share their personal stories and help us feelconnected and supported. When we show our own vulnerable side, we build realbonds and realize we're not alone.

Once you've identified areas where visibility challenges exist, you can concentrate onhealing those aspects and growing more comfortable.

Guiding Principles for Navigating this Transformative Process:

Embrace fears as opportunities to be curious and understand the lessons involved insituations and challenges. Grow in self-awareness and show up authentically. Shiftyour focus away from self and toward supporting others, embracing life'suncertainties, and learning from them. Strive to be vulnerable and genuine, allowingothers to see the real you without fear of judgment. Embrace imperfection andunderstand that progress matters most.

Accept yourself unconditionally and build self-confidence through the principles ofpositive psychology, focusing on your genuine strengths and talents. Transform yourinner world to overcome blockages, traumas, fears, imposter syndrome, and self-doubt that arise with increased visibility. Practice self-compassion and understanding,gradually progressing to overcome challenges and embrace authenticity by stayingtrue to yourself.

Purposefully make yourself visible to others, seeking and providing support andencouragement while embracing growth and learning through failure. Celebrateprogress and accomplishments, and establish strong and healthy boundaries.Practice mindfulness for self-awareness and growth, approach situations with anopen mind and adaptability, surrender with trust in the divine, have patience, detachfrom the outcome and enjoy the journey without having high expectations.

Develop resilience to persistently express yourself authentically through challenges,acknowledging feelings without judgment.

Remember, your worth isn't based onexternal validation. Shift your perspective on challenges and practice self-love andself-compassion to build resilience. Establish strong boundaries to foster self-respectand authenticity. Cultivate a supportive community that acknowledges andcelebrates your progress, reinforcing your visibility journey by celebrating progress.

Celebrate every step toward authentic self-expression, regardless of size. Holdyourself accountable by setting visibility targets, such as networking events or onlineposts, and share your plans to stay committed. Craft memorable experiences that gobeyond events, as clients desire meaningful interactions and exceptionalexperiences, not just transactions. Remember that anonymity is the true obstacle, notyour competitors.

To spark interest, be captivating and intriguing. Guide individuals in cultivatingresilience and adaptability, equipping them with tools to navigate obstacles withgrace and determination while remembering that every individual is unique and willhave their own healing and growth timeline that feels right to them. You are not hereto change anyone. Change is a call from within, and self-empowerment comes withpersonal responsibility. Showcase your expertise in fostering emotional strength andperseverance – essential qualities for embracing visibility and achieving success. Setboundaries assertively to ensure well-being while maintaining visibility.

You are the boss of your visibility.

You get to decide how much you show and share. It's okay to take breaks and haveyour own space. Life is a mix of enjoying the spotlight and having quiet moments.You have the power to choose when you want to shine and when you want to take astep back. Your choices matter, and they empower you to find the right balancebetween being out there and enjoying your own time. It's your journey, and you're incontrol.

In your personal relationships, you can choose to open up and share your thoughtsand feelings when you're ready. You can decide when you want to express yourvulnerabilities and when you need your space for introspection and growth.Remember, true connections are built on authenticity; you have the right to choosewho you want to reveal yourself and your vulnerability at your own pace.

In your career, you have the freedom to decide when to showcase your skills andaccomplishments. You can choose when to take on leadership roles or step back tolearn and observe. Your visibility at work is a tool that you can use strategically toadvance and contribute.

Social environments offer you a stage where you can shine your light and engagewith others. But you also have the prerogative to retreat when you need moments ofsolitude. The power to decide how much of your social life you want to reveal isentirely yours.

In your personal growth journey, you determine how much of your progress andtransformation you want to share with the world. It's your prerogative to celebrateyour victories and milestones, and equally important to honour your private momentsof self-discovery.

The digital world, including social media, is an arena where you can curate youronline presence according to your comfort. You can choose when to engage andwhen to disconnect, aligning your virtual visibility with your personal values.

The essence of this empowerment lies in understanding that you are not obligated tobe visible in every single aspect of life. It's about knowing that you have theautonomy to choose when you want to be open and when you want to retreat. Yourjourney is unique, and you have the authority to shape it as you see fit.

Embrace the freedom to reveal and retreat as you see fit. Your healing visibility is ajourney guided by your choices. Shine when ready and find comfort in quietmoments when needed. This is your path, and you're in control.

Author's Biography

As a catalyst for transformation, Marcela's approach is grounded in a deep understanding of the complexities of human emotions and experiences. She works unwaveringly to help people overcome blockages, pain, suffering, trauma, and toxic relationships. Through this process, individuals can realign with their life's purpose, manifest their desires, and evolve spiritually, resulting in a profound transformation in their relationships, intimacy, and overall zest for life.

Marcela is a Love and Relationship Healer, recognised by the American Board of Sexology as a Sexologist, Medical Intuitive, Skilled Helper, and a qualified professional practitioner in Cognitive Behavioural Therapy, Counselling Skills, Mindfulness, and Neuro-Linguistic Programming. She is also a Spiritual Medium, Artist, Holistic Therapist, and Teacher. Marcela has a natural talent for sharing her knowledge and wisdom in powerful and captivating ways.

Guided by love, integrity, compassion, growth, and service, she is committed to authentic relationships, creativity, and resilience. With a strong foundation in Business Management and a diverse career spanning sectors like Banking, Maritime, Oil & Gas, Fashion, and Government, she merges corporate insights with transformative healing. Marcela focuses on guiding individuals through self-discovery and empowerment.

Covering various aspects such as personal and spiritual growth, building resilience, improving communication skills, addressing limiting beliefs and self-sabotage, resolving conflicts, cultivating authentic leadership, promoting mindfulness and well-being, boosting confidence and assertiveness, adapting to change and uncertainty, enhancing creativity and innovation, honing intuition and decision-making skills, balancing work-life and personal life, leading with empathy and compassion, managing energy, preventing burnout, aligning business values with personal principles, and strengthening resilience in leadership, Marcela transforms challenges into opportunities.

Marcela is known as a Soulful Inspirational Speaker, and her talks include: 'Healing Visibility_From Unseen to Unforgettable.', Embracing Imperfection to Elevate Self-esteem, 'Strategies to Nurture Your Inner Critic.' and 'Love, Intimacy, and Ways to Strengthen Relationships.' She has also shared the stage with Deepak Chopra, Les Brown, Neal Donald Walsch, Elena Cardone, Dr. Joe Vitale (from 'The Secret') and many other world thought leaders, and is the host of two engaging talk shows: 'Shifts, Choices & Laughter Lifts,' and its Portuguese counterpart, 'Decisões e Risadas,' set to launch in March 2024. With guests from diverse walks of life, these shows share valuable insights and focus on the transformative power of making positive choices, bringing joy, and uplifting spirits.

She is an International Best Selling author and her publications include 'Awaken to Embrace Vulnerability and Sexuality' as well as her collaboration on 'Business, Life and the Universe Volume 9' with Dr. Joe Vitale and Vol.11 with authors Ken Honda (Happy Money) and James Redfield (Celestine Prophecy). These works embody her life experiences, showcasing proven tools and insights shared passionately, captivating readers with profound wisdom and powerful delivery, reflecting her life experiences and offering proven tools for self discovery. Marcela is currently immersed in the creation of her next book with more to follow soon!

Expertise:

Modern Applied Psychology & NLP

Counselling Skills

Love, Life, Intimacy

Relationships

Medical Intuitive

Mindfulness

Reiki Master

Sexology

Spiritual Development

www.ingramcontent.com/pod-product-compliance
Lightning Source LLC
Chambersburg PA
CBHW051244020426
42333CB00025B/3048